Abused, Used, and Abandoned

Now Valued and Loved

Abused, Used, and Abandoned

Now Valued and Loved

A True Story

Kelly Clayner

Abused, Used, and Abandoned, Now Valued and Loved: A True Story

Unless otherwise noted Scripture quotations are taken from THE HOLY BIBLE, NEW INTERNATIONAL VERSION®, NIV® Copyright © 1973, 1978, 1984, 2011 by Biblica, Inc.® Used by permission. All rights reserved worldwide.

Some names have been changed to protect identity.

Printed by Createspace, an Amazon.com company

Janet Atkins, cover image
Melissa Hughes, editor
Joanne Liang, design

This book is written to those who have been abused, used, and abandoned . . . and cast aside as victims. If one person reads this book and finds love, redemption, and forgiveness in the One who truly knows them—their Creator—my effort has not been in vain.

CONTENTS

ACKNOWLEDGMENTS

Some time ago I heard a man say, "Anyone can write, it is the editors you need to give credit to as they 'fine tune' what you have written." I thought I'd include that remark here because that will certainly be true of my writing.

I want to thank many who have encouraged me, after I've shared parts of my story with them, by saying "You should write your story." Those remarks I stored away in my mind for years and years until recently a friend said, "Kelly, may I write your story?" Together we began to do this until the thought continually came to my mind, "Kelly, write your own story."

When Roy, my husband of thirty-four years, asked me to marry him, I told him my past life and he still wanted to marry me, saying, "If God wants to use your past, we must let Him." From our beginning, his words have empowered me to use my story for good. My gratitude also goes to Sonya who wanted to write my story but encouraged me to do it by saying, "No one can write the story better than the one who lived it." My thanks also go to Barbara who gave me her honest opinion as to whether this story was to go further than my computer and to Hannah who gave some good suggestions and wrote the first and third appendices. Special thanks go to Melissa who edited my book and to Joanne who did the typesetting and all that was necessary to see my book get into print.

INTRODUCTION

You may have picked up this book because the word *abuse* caught your attention, having experienced real trauma in your own life—though my abuse may differ from what you experienced. I am going to tell a story now of another person with whom you may identify. Not so long ago I was with this young woman who had been abused in inconceivable ways. This is her story, her name changed to protect her identity.

Janini was born and brought up in the far west of Nepal. She is one of six siblings in her family. Her father was a laborer, spending his working hours breaking rocks with a hammer into small stones. He was an alcoholic, and when Janini's mother found out that her husband had tuberculosis, she married another man. When Janini's father died, her family situation deteriorated, and she went to live with her grandmother.

Some years later Janini was married, but her husband didn't take care of her, so she returned to her grandmother. The stigma of leaving her husband caused the people in her village to ignore her. Janini was unhappy with her grandmother so she left her and spent four months living in the forest nearby.

One day, she met a man called Kabiram who offered her a job in a foreign country. He promised her a better life, in which people would love her if she had money. Janini agreed to go with him, without telling anyone.

Kabiram taught Janini every word she was to say, in response to whatever questions were asked of her, especially at the border of India and Nepal. When they arrived in Nepalgung, Kabi-ram took Janini to Maya's house where there were four girls, and together they crossed the border, ending up in Mumbai (Bombay), India. Contrary to the deal, they were kept locked in a room and were never allowed to go outside. Each night they were given a pill before sleeping, and when they woke up in the morning they found themselves naked. Over the next three months the girls were sexually abused and physically tortured. Life was hell. Janini, with a duplicate passport made for her, was trafficked to Saudi Arabia, where she was engaged in housework, but even there she was sexually abused on a regular basis. She was often drugged by being given chocolate, which put her into an unconscious state. She couldn't tolerate it any more but when she tried to resist, her life was threatened.

Eventually, when her owner decided she was no longer useful to him, he sent her back to Mumbai. When she met the police there, instead of offering her support, they sent her back to the border of India/Nepal. Janini was fourteen years old and pregnant.

After this treatment and horrendous abuse, one might conclude that her life was over; nothing and no one could possibly put her life back together again.

If I was to end Janini's story there, this would be a sad story indeed. Towards the end of this book I will return to Janini again, and we will see where she is now.

Abuse is abuse, whatever shape or form it takes. At its core, it is the dehumanizing treatment of one person by another, the use of power and control to intimidate and harm someone. I've written this book because there is *hope* for each one of us and that hope comes through the person of Jesus Christ. Many people use "Jesus" or "Christ" as a swear word, and I've often wondered "Why His name of all names?" What so many don't know is that He, of all people, is for real and loves you so much that He died for you and for me. He died an excruciating death and knows intimately the pain we carry. Not only that, He overcame hate, terror, and death with His life.

Yes, Jesus, celebrated at Christmas, came into the world to be the Savior of all humankind, and sadly most people don't know it. Stay with me now and read my story—having been sexually abused as a child, put down, humiliated, ridiculed, and later left riddled with guilt and shame and then abandoned, I wondered what would become of me. Let me begin my story and get to the day I awakened to my value and to the love of the only One who really knows what it means to love. That was forty years ago. I will never forget my start in life and from where I have come. Now my greatest desire is to tell those who are in a helpless state of mind, or even so desperate that they feel life is not worth living. Life is indeed worth living when you know for whom and why you are living.

Early Years

1
CHILDHOOD

Even as a child I wondered what we were all doing here on earth. I believed God was "up there" somewhere. I wanted to make more sense of our existence, but I couldn't. Looking back, I'm glad I had a reason to ask these questions. There were times when I'd fall on my knees and ask God to help me.

My mother and father were both alcoholics, and when they were drunk I had nowhere else to go but God. I have read and heard that if you had a bad father image, your understanding of God wouldn't be much better. But that was not so with me. I believed God was the Creator of heaven and earth as far back as I can remember. I had no religious instruction in my home, yet my parents did baptize me as a baby, because it was the "thing" to do for a so-called Christian family. Other than my baptism, we never went to church as a family.

So much of our living environment as children has a huge effect on how we grow into adults. By the time I was fourteen, I was smoking cigarettes and drinking whiskey. My parents encouraged me to smoke and drink so I couldn't tell them not to. By the time I was sixteen, I was smoking twenty cigarettes a day and did so for the next ten years of my life. When I did drink whiskey on rare occasions, I added orange juice, coke, or coffee. Whiskey was in plentiful supply in my home, but thankfully I never became addicted to alcohol—maybe because I saw what alcohol did to my parents and I didn't want to end up like them. So why did my parents end up alcoholics? It is only fair to share a little of their story.

2
MY PARENTS

My father was born in 1918 in Sutton, south of London, one of three boys. The eldest of them died at fourteen years old. This was not easy for my father, who was only eight years old at the time. He told me often enough how much he had loved Peter, his brother, who died from a ruptured appendix. Without penicillin in those days, Peter didn't have a chance.

My father, after his education, went into the Royal Navy. While in the navy he married a Canadian woman, but that marriage, for whatever reason, ended in divorce. He ranked as a navigation officer before his uncle contacted the Admiralty, after the Second World War, to ask them to release his nephew from the navy to work in the family business as a merchant of tea and coffee.

My father had no interest in working in the family business and would have preferred to stay in the navy. His father was of the Victorian era and in those days sons and daughters just did what their parents or other family members told them to do. My guess is, while in the navy, the drinking set in.

My father was a womanizer and soon after my parents were married, he began to stay out all night. I heard him say on more than a few occasions when he was drunk, "Put a sack over their heads, and they are all the same." I was only a child when I heard him say that, but I can hear him to this day.

Before I was about twelve, I went looking for something in his bureau and found pictures, which judging by today's pornography were tame, but they were still pornographic. I was horrified but told no one I had seen them.

As is the case in every dysfunctional family, my father had some positive traits; he was a good cook when he was sober, which he probably learned from the cook who was employed in his childhood home.

My father chain-smoked from the moment he got out of bed in the morning, managing to inhale at least sixty cigarettes a day. After coming from London on the train at around 6:30 p.m., my father would go straight to a pub and often stay there until 9:00 at night before coming home. My mother always managed to cook dinner and kept it warm for him to eat when he eventually came home.

On the weekends, my father would start drinking whiskey as early as 10:30 a.m., taking his whiskey into the bathroom while shaving. It may be no surprise that I did a lot of housework as a child, and that work included emptying the endless ash trays, even the one in the bathroom. He went to the pub Saturday mornings and somehow managed to do the weekend shopping. After lunch, he would have to sleep off the effects of the morning alcohol before he went out again at 5:30 p.m. to start the evening drinking session. In those days, pubs were closed from 2:00 to 5:30 p.m. He didn't come home until 10:00 or 11:00 p.m.

One night he knocked on our front door and said, "I drove the car into a lamp post," then pulled out a half bottle of whiskey from his jacket pocket and, holding it in my face, smugly joked, "But this didn't get broken."

I knew it was a miracle that my father never killed anyone though he so often drove when he was drunk. He lost his license three times. Then he took taxis to get to pubs and continued with his daily drinking routine. Not surprisingly, we didn't have much money because it was spent on alcohol.

As a wedding present to my mother and father, my father's parents bought them a three-bedroom house. When my father had drunk all the money away, he mortgaged their house. When his parents heard of this, they thought this was shameless and paid off the mortgage. My father mortgaged the house again a few years later when he ran out of money—this time without his parents finding out (or perhaps they had died by that time).

My mother was born in Bombay, India, as it was called then, in the year 1914. My brother told me recently that our grandfather on our mother's side ran away from home at fourteen and found himself on a ship as a cabin boy. By the time he was twenty-one he had sailed around the world three times on tall sail ships. He went up the ranks and became Bombay's harbor dredging master and did that job for thirty-one years.

On one of the few occasions my grandfather went back to England he met Edith, married her and took her back to India. When Iris, my mother, was five years old, her mother took her back to England on a ship and placed her in a convent in Brentwood in Essex, England. My grandmother returned to India. My mother told me that the Mother Superior of the convent cared for her as her own child.

On two occasions before Iris completed her education at seventeen, her mother went to visit her while she was in England. Since my mother was brought up by nuns, she had some understanding of Catholicism, evidenced by her request to me as an adult: "When I die, pray me out of purgatory." How sad to think this was where you were going after death.

When my mother finished school, she sailed to Bombay. It was the time of the Raj, when the British ruled India, and British officers flocked round this young and beautiful woman at formal parties. This sudden change of lifestyle was a stark contrast from the convent where she grew up in England. She remained in

India for three years and then returned to England and trained as a beautician.

My mother eventually rented a salon and had her own business. During these years, she was taken in and convinced by Spiritualism. Before I was a teenager, she told me she had guides who basically controlled her. She married during the Second World War and became pregnant. Frank, her husband, was killed in action, and on hearing this news my mother aborted their baby. What an emotional trauma this must have been for my mother. I can only imagine that, with one heartbreak after another or with some bad influence, the addiction of alcohol set in deeper and deeper.

My mother was in her mid-thirties when she met my father. After their marriage, she desperately wanted a baby. She became pregnant with my brother. It was a hard delivery, so much so that she nearly died. My father told me that her doctor said to him, "If you want to kill your wife, get her pregnant, she will never live through another delivery." Wrong, of course, otherwise I wouldn't be writing this story. But she did go through a terrible time having me and apparently nearly did die. I've sometimes wondered whether the abortion she had caused her such difficulties in having my brother and me. My mother gave birth to me in 1951, two and a half years after my brother, when she was thirty-eight.

From as far back as I can remember my parents drank whiskey. When it was unbearable for me as a child I used to run to my bedroom, fall to my knees, and ask God to make them stop drinking whiskey. He never did, but somehow, I never became angry with God. In fact, I felt a comfort in talking to God at these times. I somehow believed God did know me and that He was watching over my life.

My mother also started drinking early in the day, with a cigarette wedged between her lips, as she washed clothes at the kitchen sink or did other chores around the house. She did have a spin dryer which helped reduce her tedious workload, if ever so slightly, before she hung all the wash on a line.

She too had to sleep off the alcohol in the afternoons before starting to drink again, watching the television while mending clothes and sometimes darning a few holes in my father's socks, as well as cooking an evening meal. Sadly, my mother often didn't get dressed and hung around in a stained dressing gown all day. That always bothered me—I thought it slovenly. And all the while her lungs were inhaling forty cigarettes a day.

There were occasions, few as they were, when my mother had to dress up and go somewhere, and when she did, she looked lovely. I remember going up to London with her, and as soon as we arrived at Victoria Station, before going anywhere else, she went to a hotel bar and had a large whiskey. There was just no end to it.

While my father became pathetic, crude, and eventually passed out when he was drunk, my mother became belligerent and nasty. In my mother's sober moments, however, she was lovely. I knew she loved me, and if only she had not been an alcoholic, we would have had such a nice mother and daughter relationship.

On Saturday afternoons, while my dad was snoring away or in the evenings when he was at the pubs, together my mother and I would watch movie after movie. Sometimes I wanted to cuddle with her so much that, as big as I was, I sat on her lap. Those are the memories I hold in my heart of my mother.

I've told you a bit about my parents, not to disrespect them— though they did kill themselves with cirrhosis of the liver and cancer due to about fifty years of smoking and alcohol abuse—but with two reasons in mind. One reason is that we become what we are very much due to our heritage and family background, and if our parents do not raise us as God intends, then all hell can break loose for us.

In my mother's case, she was abandoned by her parents. What resulted was that my mother was confused by a Catholic school upbringing and further by Spiritualism, which dragged her down and gave her no peace or joy, but left her to seek inebriation to escape her misery. Having an alcoholic, womanizing husband, living with the memory that her first husband was killed in the Second World War, and possibly regretting the abortion of her first baby did not help her unhappy state of mind during my childhood years.

At the age of eight, my father saw the death of his beloved fourteen-year-old brother. He wanted to remain in a career he liked, but was told in no uncertain terms that he was to resign and do what his father and uncle told him to do. Could resentment have set in when he was forced to leave the navy?

Whatever his emotional or mental state, he drank alcohol and became addicted. Being irresponsible with women and money drove him to the whiskey bottle, to forget the pain, no doubt, of not doing what he wanted to do, of not being a responsible husband and father.

So these were my parents and I have shared as much about them as I can remember, as painful as these memories are. There may be times when we want to bury our past, never to talk about it to anyone, and live in denial that it all happened to us. There have been occasions when someone would say to me, "Oh, but you wouldn't understand because my father (or mother) is an alcoholic." Then I can kindly respond saying, "But I can and do understand; not only was my father an alcoholic but my mother was as well."

3
SEXUALLY ABUSED

More than anything I remember of my childhood, I wish to this day I could eradicate the memory of my father sexually abusing me. The sexual abuse happened when my father was sober first thing in the morning.

As a little girl, I would wake early and climb into my parents' bed. When I was around eight years old and I was in their bed, my father started to touch my body all over, and it wasn't long until I was experiencing multiple orgasms.

My mother was fast asleep and knew nothing of what her husband was doing to me, their little girl. The feeling was nice, more than nice, so much so I went back into their bed to experience this nice feeling on more than a few occasions. I am thankful my father never penetrated me, but he did kiss me. I didn't like that and didn't want him to do it.

My father took my innocence from me. As young as I was, did I even know what innocence meant? This was the beginning of a downward spiral toward a bottomless pit for me, until one day I would fall on my knees nineteen years later and cry to God and say over and over again, "Please help me, God, I am so sorry,"—by then I had made a lot of bad choices—"please help me." And He did. But that was many years later, and as a child I still had to face each day in my vulnerable situation.

When I was nine years old, I was parceled off to boarding school with the memory of what my father had done to me.

When we think of *abuse*, our minds possibly go to sexual abuse. There are, however, other kinds of abuse. One form is when we are not treated properly, made to feel less than human, or blamed for problems over which we have no control, and that is emotional and mental abuse. I endured emotional and mental abuse for the next few years of my life. Unlike some of you reading this story, I was never physically abused—many survivors of abuse never are.

Growing Pains

4
SCHOOL DAYS

I can never remember my parents reading me a book, even though I did have a few children's books in my bedroom. I went to a local primary school, riding my bicycle at a very young age. When that school closed down I was only nine, and I was packed off to boarding school. Raven's Croft School made an exception to admit me at nine years old because the starting age was ten.

Soon after I was placed in the youngest class I was called to the front of the classroom to read. I was a poor reader. Classmates snickered, whispering to one another, "Can't she read?" Humiliated, I sat down in my seat knowing that schoolwork was going to be a nightmare. I can't remember one word to this day.

My mind wandered in class. Our school was built on top of a cliff overlooking the south coast of England. Sitting by a window I'd often find myself gazing out at the ocean. Who knows where my mind drifted, but it certainly wasn't listening to and learning what the teachers were teaching.

I was a hopeless note-taker so I had to get help from other classmates who were kind enough to work with me. End of term was the worst, when the student body was lined up in the gymnasium and we all had to stand to hear the headmistress, Miss Roberts, read aloud for all to hear the placement of every single student in each class.

Two girls in my class fought for first place every semester, and I fought not to take last place in the class, but invariably I did. How humiliating it was for me to stand there and for the whole school to know I was at the bottom of my class at the end of most school years. Thinking about it now, they probably couldn't have cared less, just so that they weren't the one at the bottom of their class.

I did have two things in my favor that helped me survive school. One was that I enjoyed sports. I was selected to play on the netball and tennis teams. I also had some nice friends, even though one girl really didn't like me and did all she could to make my life miserable.

One of my good friends, Jennifer, is still a close friend to this day. Seven years ago, when I was in England staying with my brother and sister-in-law, I turned sixty. My brother said he would be happy to throw a birthday party for me, but I declined and said, "No, thank you, I only want two of my friends for dinner," one being Jennifer, my friend who was in the same class as me at school.

While I was at boarding school, my parents were allowed to come and take me out for the day on Sunday after church, twice in a term. Frankly, I dreaded them coming, as I knew they would have stopped at a pub on the way to school and anticipated them having had one too many before we even started my supposedly nice day out with them.

The first stop once I had been picked up was to a pub. Being under age to go into a pub, I stayed in the car with a coke and a packet of crisps. We eventually went somewhere for lunch and then for a drive to Beachy Head on the south coast or took a walk along the promenade or went on the pier. After tea in a café, they dropped me back to school.

I mentioned earlier that my parents never took me to church, but it was mandatory at this boarding school. Why me, I don't know—but I was asked to go up to the altar at this Anglican Church, light the candles before the service began, and read scriptures from the Bible during the service. I liked doing this and even felt somewhat important. However, when the sermon was being preached, my mind wandered and after it was done I remember thinking, "Oh dear, I didn't listen to one word the vicar said."

Neither my days out nor my days in at school were a picnic in the park. I remember one instance at school when I was ten. I had done something wrong and a prefect, a senior student with the privileges to "get tough" with the young students, punished me by making me miss watching television on a Saturday afternoon and sending me off to a piano practice room.

There I had to stay until I had learned a sonnet, fourteen lines of Shakespeare, word perfect. It took me a long time to get those fourteen lines in my head, which didn't make much sense to me, and repeat them back to her perfectly, but I did it, because she would not relent. The prefect was not kind and showed me no mercy.

Raven's Croft was supposed to be a Christian school. All students and staff would walk into the gymnasium and attend assembly every morning before classes. Miss Roberts, the principal, led assembly by playing hymns on the piano, followed by a short prayer ending in Jesus' Name, amen. I also recall the student body watching "The Ten Commandments" on a Saturday night in the gymnasium. That was the sum total of anything to do with God or Jesus that I remember from school.

The following morning after watching the "Ten Commandments" I woke up with chicken pox. It was just before the end of term. I was delighted to see the spots all over my body since I would miss end of term exams, which saved me from more humiliation knowing I would probably fail most of them anyway, if not all of them. It was decided by the matron to call my parents and to have them come and take me home before I started an epidemic in the school. As luck would have it, the day before I woke up with chicken pox a friend gave me the book *Gone with the Wind*.

I looked at it in amazement and thumbed through it, seeing that it had more than a thousand pages, even though the print was reasonably large. That book was a lifesaver. I was now about thirteen, and I loved being at home in bed, reading the best book I had ever read, even though it took me much longer than most other children of my age to read. A movie was made of this book and still to this day, "Gone With The Wind" remains one of my favorite movies.

I was at Raven's Croft School for five years before it closed down. Two of my friends, one I've already mentioned, Jennifer, decided that the three of us would do all we could to go to another school together. As it happened, the three of us did end up at the same school, Hurst Lodge in Sunningdale in Berkshire.

Jennifer's father and mother were divorced. She told me years later that she envied me because my parents were together, while I envied her as her mother lived in what seemed to me like a mansion, and on the grounds there were stables. Jennifer and her brother had their own ponies.

On one occasion Jennifer invited me to spend the weekend with her at her mother's home. I had riding lessons at school, so Jennifer let me ride her pony, and I thought Jennifer had the best life. I had seen Jennifer's father on a couple of occasions and thought him a very handsome man.

In the summer of 1965 when I was fourteen, Jennifer's dad was taking Jennifer and her brother to the south of France for a few days holiday, and he told Jennifer she could bring a friend. Jennifer invited me, and I couldn't have been happier. Her father owned a convertible Rolls Royce. Did I feel the big shot sitting in the back seat of a convertible Rolls Royce all the way to the south of France!

After checking in at the hotel, Jennifer went into our en suite bathroom when her father gently sat me on the bed, laid me down, and kissed me on the lips. I was so shocked to think that at any moment Jennifer would come out of the bathroom and see her father kissing me. Just the thought was too much to bear. Whether I was able to push him away or he felt that time was up, I was on my feet before Jennifer came out of the bathroom while her dad lay calmly on the bed. I was definitely in shock.

The next day Jennifer's dad said, "I have business in London, so I will fly back now and be back here tomorrow evening!" Can you imagine that he left his daughter and her friend, both of us just fourteen and his thirteen-year-old son alone in the south of France and thought it was okay? He did return the next day (thank goodness), and I can't remember much more about that trip other than that Jennifer's father did not touch or kiss me again, but was nice to me and acted as if nothing had happened. I never told anyone about that kiss.

I was at Hurst Lodge School for just a little less than two years when my father told me while I was at home, "There is no more money to send you to a private boarding school." I don't know why it was in the bathroom of our house, but I remember just standing there, thinking, "What is to become of me? I don't have a qualification to my name, so what will I do?"

I thought to myself that one day I would take myself back to school and qualify for something. My father's older brother, chairman of the family business, paid for me to go to secretarial school since there was no talk of me going from a private school to a local school to endure more humiliation, for which I was thankful.

At sixteen I was enrolled into Mrs. Wolf's Secretarial School. Mrs. Wolf lived up to her name and was quite scary. The shorthand course was wasted on me as I couldn't keep up with the shorthand dictation. Looking back, I think I was dyslexic, and probably still am, so that may have been why learning at school was so hard for me. I did, however, enjoy the typing course.

Mrs. Wolf said, "If you look at the typing keys while you do your drills in learning the keys, you will never 'touch type,' and for those of you who do not look at the keys, you will be the ones who end up the fastest typists."

I was learning on the old-fashioned typewriters, and if you made a mistake there was no "back space" to erase your mistake. We had to use an eraser so that we invariably ended up rubbing a hole in the paper and had to start again. I took her at her word and decided not to look at the keys while learning and I actually achieved something by being able to touch type at the end of that school year. Hence, typing my story on a computer now is an enjoyable task for me, having learned to type over fifty years ago. I'm especially glad for the "back space" key!

5
DIMITRI

During my sixteenth year, while I was at secretarial training I was introduced to Dimitri. I was attracted to Dimitri, as he was to me. His father was English and his mother Greek. By the time we met, his parents were divorced. His mother married again to an American.

Dimitri was my first boyfriend. He always looked expensively dressed and was one of those guys who would make heads turn. He owned a convertible, an Alfa Romeo sports car, which was an added attraction to this already attractive guy. He was two years older than me and had finished private school by the time I met him.

As we spent more and more time together, I thought I was in love with him. He would come to my parents' home, and my mother, though she liked him, knew that this relationship could only end in disaster. He was definitely a ladies' man. His family life was a far cry from my alcoholic home but he didn't seem to mind and accepted a whiskey soon after he entered our home.

If my mother was right about one thing, it was about Dimitri; our relationship was doomed from the beginning. Amazingly though, our relationship lingered on and off for the next four years. Sometimes he would go to Florida to be with his mother, and I missed him terribly. He wrote me a few letters and I hung on to every loving word he wrote trying to convince myself I was the one for him. In the back of my mind I knew this was a false hope I had created, and yet still I clung on hoping upon hope that I really meant something to him. There came a time towards the end of our relationship that I finally woke up to the fact that I meant not much more to him than his own sexual gratification. Looking back, those were four years of being used.

After a year of knowing him, I still felt insecure, but I told my parents that they could decide between me and the whiskey. They chose the whiskey, so I left home and went to live with Dimitri in London. We did go to visit my parents on occasions and even stayed the night, sleeping in the same bed; my parents didn't mind.

Travel and Jobs

6
FRANCE

During the four years of our relationship, I actually went to France twice to get away from Dimitri. It was becoming a love/hate relationship. I couldn't live with him and thought I couldn't live without him. Once I went to Marseille as an au pair, staying with a family and looking after the children. After about a month, Dimitri said he was missing me and told me he wanted me to come back to him. I told him to send me a telegram telling me my grandmother was dying so the family for whom I was au pairing would let me return to England. They did. This, of course, was a terrible thing to do, as my grandmother was fine, but only something drastic could break my agency agreement.

Not long after I was back with Dimitri, he started to see other women. This time I left for Paris. I lived near the Champs-Elysees and was again an au pair to an American family. They had twin boys of four and a nine-year-old daughter. The father was an American diplomat. The mother was an amateur tennis player and often went off to play in tournaments. We all went on one occasion to Gstaad in the mountains of Switzerland for the wife to play in a tennis tournament there.

The husband liked horse racing, and once he invited me to go with him. When he gave me this invitation, his wife was in earshot and said, "Go, you'll enjoy the races." I accepted the invitation. We were allowed to go in the enclosure where the horses walk around before the jockeys mounted their rides. The day was nothing more than a fun day out for me. He was fatherly and never made an advance towards me.

While in Paris with this family, I did have a traumatic experience. I slept in a room on the top floor of the apartment block; you might say the servants' quarters. It had glass doors that opened out onto a small balcony. That summer of 1968 was extremely hot, so I just kept the doors open while I slept. There was no window to open.

One night I was awakened from being fast asleep with a hand over my mouth. Light was coming in my room from the street lights so that I could see the man was black. I was so frightened, knowing his intent, but thankful at the same time when my nose started to bleed profusely, and once this young guy saw the blood on his hand and the blood dripping onto the sheets, he got scared and said, "Don't scream and I'll go." I didn't scream, and he bolted for the door and left.

I went down to the family and told them what had just happened to me. The husband came upstairs and knocked on the door of the guy who had climbed from his balcony onto mine. He said, "If you ever so much as look at this girl again, I will have you deported so fast you will not know what has happened to you." He got the message. However, I was a bit nervous in case he had "friends" who would "do me in." Thankfully, that never happened, although I did see him in the street one day.

I always wanted to learn French and thought while I was in France I should go to the Alliance Françoise School for international students. I enrolled feeling nervous and insecure without much hope of learning anything. I turned up on the first day to be seated next to a Mexican guy who was shorter than I was and had black oily hair. His name was Rodriguez. He was soft-spoken with a kind personality and spoke English well.

Outside after class one day I noticed he was unlocking his huge, shiny, black motorbike, and once astride it he said to me, "Would you like to go with me to visit Versailles?"

Versailles was the home of King Louis XIV. I had seen pictures of this beautiful palace and I had thought to myself that I would love to go visit Versailles while I was in Paris. I accepted this invitation and he said, "We'll go on the bike."

I'd never been on a motorbike before but the thrill of it would be worth every bit of the adventure. Versailles is about an hour from Paris. We had a wonderful day out, and I have never forgotten this person who befriended me. In fact, he was the only friend I had when I was in Paris.

As I started to get to know this young man, who was about my age, he brought Jesus into the conversation. I wondered how anyone could speak so freely of Jesus when He had died on a cross more than two thousand years ago. I actually felt uneasy and irritated when he talked about Jesus as his Savior and Lord.

Rodriguez invited me to his home to meet his family. His father was a diplomat from Mexico, and all his family welcomed me into their home. I did not feel threatened, and I didn't have any feeling that Rodriguez liked me for gratifying his own sexual desire. Just the opposite, he was different and I felt safe with him and cared for by his family.

Missing me again, Dimitri came to Paris to see me with his father. One evening after dinner it was suggested we go to an exhibition. Not having the slightest idea what they had in mind, I just said, "Yes, let's."

Foolishly, I had agreed to something without knowing what I was getting into. I couldn't believe where I ended up, watching live sex. I was eighteen years old. I was stunned. I wanted to run out of that place, but I just stood there, powerless to move.

The exhibition was all very cynical with young, good-looking performers. They came in, did what they did, and left the room.

Dimitri left with his father back to London after a few days. I stayed on in Paris the rest of the summer and returned to England.

I went back to live with my parents. Soon after I returned from Paris I took a job in Balham in London, which, back in the late 1960s, was not a safe area for young women. My first and only typing job was doing invoices in an automobile repair shop. I don't think I lasted two weeks. I didn't like the job, so I left without pay. I received a card from Rodriguez saying he was praying for me; I didn't need prayer, or so I thought. But in fact, in hindsight I never needed prayer more than during the next few years of my life.

Nothing much changed after going back to live in my parent's home, only that I was older, all of nineteen. I'd made a lot of mistakes while away from home so I was thankful that they would have me back.

7
MODELING AND SPAIN

It was suggested to me, "Why don't you do modeling? You have a pretty face." I believed what I'd heard, that models have pretty faces but no brains; so I thought I'd fit the bill and gave it a try.

I did a four-week modeling course in London and then joined a modeling agency, also in London, and became self-employed. My brother and I were both living at home at this time. He had a job in London and drove up every day. So, for the next two years my brother drove me to London to where I had a modeling job. It was a significant time to spend with my brother, and he looked out for his little sis.

I had a couple of photographic jobs, but I mainly did shows at fashion houses for buyers from shops to select their seasons' collections. The best thing that came out of my modeling days, which lasted two years, was my friendship with Jane. We had joined the same agency and were both employed to work for some of the same fashion houses.

We struck up a friendship that led us to go to Spain together on holiday in the summer of 1971. Jane had a friend who wanted to come, and that friend brought another friend. The four of us paid for a week's holiday, flight and hotel included, to go to Torremolinos. It was a cheap package deal, and we had no intention of being on the return flight home a week later.

Before the week was up, we found an apartment near the beach, one large room with four beds, a small kitchen, and bathroom. We were good for two months, as that was our intention. How we were going to get back to England from Spain we left to fate, but we were not going to let that worry us and spoil our two-month vacation, spent primarily on the beach every day, swimming in the ocean and getting a sun tan.

Money was a bit of an issue for Jane and me, so, when offered jobs as "Go-Go Girls" at a nightclub, we took it. It was not a seedy, dingy place. It was a bar with a dance floor, but it wasn't crowded or focused on luring old men.

In the late 1960s the pop music was great—in my opinion, music to which one could actually dance. We wore well-covered tops and a sarong, a long cross-over tie skirt, over our shorts. Jane and I thought we were pretty cool dancing on a stage.

One of the other girls met a Spaniard quite soon after getting settled into our apartment. He seemed to be a nice guy, and she was happy with her new boyfriend. He had a speedboat which she enjoyed, as did we, when we had the invitation to join them.

I too met a guy, much older than myself, maybe by fifteen years, and he was wealthy. He invited me to Cannes in the south of France for a weekend. He offered to pay for my flight ticket and book me into a hotel if I wanted to go. Did I think for one moment he was doing this because he liked me? How foolish I was if I thought so.

I didn't find him attractive, but he seemed like a nice person. I knew the others were a bit wary of this invitation, but I thought, why not? Who wouldn't want to go to the French Riviera, which was certainly a hundred notches up from a cheap vacation like the bucket and spade brigade in Torremolinos. So, I decided to go.

I don't remember him meeting me at the airport, but I do remember him coming into my hotel room. Not long after, I found myself in the bathroom thinking, "I think I have just been raped." No, he didn't like me for who I was, but had one thing in mind, to have sex with me, and would probably boast to his friends how it only cost him a flight ticket and a hotel room.

Admittedly, the hotel was beautiful. He took me to a fancy restaurant on the beach with others in company, and thankfully that is about as much as I can remember of that ordeal. I felt I had no one to blame but myself for thinking I would be respected and liked for who I was and able to just have a nice time.

Of course, it was a bad decision on my part to go on a weekend with someone I hardly knew. Other than that incident, the four of us had a good time together.

As time was drawing to a close, to get back to England, Jane and I decided to try and get a ride back with someone who had driven to Torremolinos from London. As luck would have it, a guy we met on the beach had a red, flashy Corvette Stingray convertible sports car and was heading back to London in a few days. We simply asked him, "Can we ride with you back to London?"

He said, "Sure, no problem."

Thankfully there were no strings attached.

The seating arrangement wasn't the best since it was only comfortable for two people sitting in the front two bucket seats. But to get home with only the cost of food and a one-night stay in a bed and breakfast was a good deal.

Jane and I took turns squishing in the back, in what was not even a seat. Luckily, we were thin in those days because if any fatter, once in, it would have been near impossible to get out!

We arrived home without hassle and thoroughly enjoyed the ride through Spain and France. For Jane and me it was back to walking the catwalk and down the path of our lifelong friendship, which continues to this day, fifty years later.

8
NURSING

I liked to work, but I didn't get enough modeling jobs so I inquired at a hospital in Epsom if they had any job that I might be able to do. The matron was kind and agreed to take me on as an extra auxiliary nurse. I fetched and carried bedpans and gave bed baths to patients who couldn't get out of bed after an operation.

One dear soul, Mary, had multiple sclerosis and was bedridden, and I often gave her bed baths. I made beds, helped patients feel comfortable, and anything else that didn't require giving out medication or injections. I was allowed to take temperatures and pulses. I felt quite proud dressed up in my nurse's uniform and cap. By now I was twenty years old.

The morning shift started at 7:00. I was very satisfied with this job, possibly because I was serving others. This nursing job was part-time; I worked there when I didn't have modeling jobs. I received a minimal salary, which was about fifty pounds sterling or $120 a week in those days.

Without thinking too much about it, I was a very flexible person, which was certainly to come in handy later on in my life. After all, one week I was fetching and carrying bedpans and the next I was modeling expensive outfits down a catwalk! One of the fashion houses I worked for was that of Susan Small, who later designed the wedding dress of Diana Spencer (the future Princess Diana).

9

THE AIRLINE

I was coming to the end of my twentieth year by now and a girl-friend from the secretarial school told me she had been accepted by British Overseas Airline Corporation (BOAC), as it was called in the early 1970s, now British Airways. She said to me, "Kelly, I'm an air hostess with BOAC, and it is a great job flying around the world, making lots of money, and you would love it."

"Yes, Julie," I replied, "I'm sure I would love it, but they wouldn't take me because I never even finished high school, let alone speak another language."

To which she replied, "Oh, never mind that, I don't speak another language either, just apply and see what happens."

I did. I applied to BOAC, had an interview, and was turned down. I remember my father saying one encouraging thing to me; he said, "Don't give up, apply to British Caledonian Airways."

This was a Scottish Independent Airline, the next biggest airline to BOAC in the UK. I applied to British Caledonian Airways just before my twenty-first birthday.

I mentioned that there were times when my parents were drunk that I used to actually kneel down and pray to God. I thought God would not give you an audience if you didn't have the right posture, and pleaded with Him for what I was asking. Now I was again on my knees asking God to give me this job as an air hostess. I believed I could do this job, and I wanted to do it.

The day came when I was to go to a posh London hotel where the airline was interviewing for air hostesses. My appointment was around 6:00 p.m. and I was one of the last applicants to be interviewed that day. Before entering into the interviewing room, I saw on the left a grand piano (the room being a ballroom of the hotel), and on the piano was a large stack of applications that said "Rejects" on top, and a small pile with the word "Acceptances." My heart sank, and all I could think was, "God, I want this job so badly, so please give it to me."

I entered the large room, and there was a lonely chair, which was obviously for me to sit in. Before me were a cabin services director, a senior air hostess, a director of the airline, and a pilot.

The panel of interviewers started to ask me questions. I can't remember all the questions they asked me, but the one I do remember is, "What makes you think you would be a good air hostess?"

I must have said something like, "I like being with people, and I like travel and variety in my life."

The one who was conducting the interview would have seen on my application in front of him or her that I didn't speak a foreign language, nor had I finished high school. Before the interview was over, I was told by one of them that I would hear within a week as to whether I was accepted or not.

When the interview was over, I certainly was not confident I would be accepted, but I just kept hoping and telling God I really wanted this job. "Please God, give me this job." I kept saying this over and over again.

Within a week of the interview, a letter from British Caledonian Airways appeared in my mailbox, and I prayed again before opening the envelope, "Please, please, please God."

To my delight, on opening the letter I read: "Dear Kelly, We have pleasure in accepting you to begin your flight training on January 17, 1972." Wow, I got the job! I was ecstatically happy that I was to start a day after my twenty-first birthday. "Thank you, thank you, God, for giving me this job that I really wanted."

If I had known then what I know now, I could imagine God saying something like this, "Kelly, you wanted this job so badly that I have given it to you, but when you find it doesn't satisfy you, I will be waiting for you to lead you on a path that will totally satisfy you for the rest of your life."

I was to see Dimitri whom I had been seeing off and on for the last four years one last time. I guess I wanted him to see me really happy and for him to know that I neither wanted nor needed him in my life anymore. I felt I was in charge of my life now that I was going to start working for an airline, travel the world, and be permanently employed with a good salary. For the first time in my life I could actually say I felt good about myself, even though I still felt insecure.

It was time to leave home again. I left my parents on better terms than I did the first time. My brother had a friend who had bought an apartment opposite a sports club just outside of London. The apartment was smart and so was the club. Greg, who owned the flat, was fine with me moving in. I bought a secondhand, white, convertible sports car and felt as though I had "made it" or that I was certainly on the "up and up."

I hadn't played tennis since school days, but since I was only in my early twenties, I thought I could take up playing the game again.

In 1974 I was so excited to be going on my first trip to Singapore. I became good friends with Geraldine, another air hostess on that flight. When we arrived in Singapore, Geraldine and I met a couple of guys who took us out for the day to an island in a speedboat and taught us to water ski.

Once I got the hang of putting my knees together under my chin, keeping my arms straight outside of my knees, and keeping afloat while the boat was starting up so the rope pulling me was taut, I just had to wait for the boat to rev up and gain speed, then I would lean forward, straighten my knees, and away I went. I'll never forget how much fun it was, going from side to side riding the waves.

These guys were really nice, and the four of us had a great day out. One of the guys was a Singaporean and the other an American. It was obvious the Singaporean liked me, and I liked him.

After this fun day out, the Singaporean asked to take me to dinner and to see a cultural show. I accepted, and I enjoyed the evening immensely. At some point during the dinner the thought came to me: I'm going to sleep with him tonight. He stayed the night in my hotel room. My flight was leaving the next evening, but he wanted to take me sightseeing the next morning and to have lunch.

We enjoyed being together but we both knew I was leaving and it was the end of our brief friendship. I boarded the flight back to London and never saw him again.

When my period didn't come the next month, I wondered, could I possibly be pregnant? A pregnancy test proved positive. How could this happen to me? Easily—I had sex right in the middle of my cycle and my IUD contraceptive had dislodged. It was as simple as that.

Abortion and Recovery

10
ABORTION

I loved babies and wanted my own one day, but not now, not when I was enjoying a job I really liked. I knew I wasn't thinking too much about it, even though I knew what I was contemplating was wrong. I justified what I was going to do by telling myself that I wasn't irresponsible because I had taken a precaution even though the contraceptive failed me. I really did believe that life began at conception, but I convinced myself that all I had in me at this stage was a blob.

I didn't know of any place to go or anyone with whom I could discuss my predicament. My parents would have been of no help whatsoever. I called my brother. He came to my flat and sympathized with me and was okay with me getting an abortion. This was so not the right time for this to happen.

I had been flying for three and a half years and had never been happier. At that time, my job was more important than my pregnancy, and I wanted nothing to come between my job and me. Even in the seventies it was still "looked down on" to be pregnant without being married.

I scheduled an abortion, but a technicians' strike in the hospital delayed it. Did this interruption of my plan lead me to seek God at this time in my life? Of course not; I just took matters into my own hands and stuck with what I had decided to do.

Once the technicians' strike was over, I was getting dangerously close to not being permitted to have an abortion. I went to the hospital and politely put that I was to have a D & C, a scraping of the womb, which essentially serves as an abortion.

I was in the hospital bed in a ward one day and discharged the next. I was put under general anesthetic so I knew nothing of what took place, thankfully. When the doctor came to see me the next day, I asked him if the baby was a boy or girl, but he wouldn't tell me. I don't know why, but I've always thought the baby was a boy.

If I had done what I knew to be right and given birth to my baby, he or she would be forty-three years old by now. Once out of the hospital I was depressed and cried continuously. I was twenty-four years old.

I had become friends with a family who didn't live too far from my parents. Penny and David had two children. The kids were little, about four and six when I first met the family. As a teenager, I loved going to their house, just being a part of their family. Sometimes I would babysit the children when Penny and David had a date, but mostly I just enjoyed being with Penny and her family.

They knew my parents and my family dynamics. They welcomed me into their home, which was always decorated beautifully. Penny was a real homemaker, gifted at the art of flower arranging. At Christmas, their house was decorated with such elegance. This family cared about me—I never felt judged by them.

In desperation, I called Penny from my flat and told her what I had done. She told me on the phone, "Pack a bag, I'm coming to get you."

They were such a support to me. When my mother and father died, David and Penny were the only people who came to their funerals. My parents didn't have friends.

11
AUSTRALIA

After a couple of weeks of "sick leave" with this dear family, it was time to get back to the skies. I was due some vacation, and my brother suggested we go to Australia together to see our distant cousins.

One of the perks of working for an airline was cheap ticket prices. With a huge discount we could afford to go to Australia. Our grandmother on our mother's side, who was at this time in her eighties, had a brother who, when he was twenty-one, had left England for Australia, never to return. He married and had three boys. By the time we went to visit them, those three boys had married and had their own children. My grandmother had kept up a correspondence with her brother's eldest son's wife.

This holiday with my brother will always remain a fond memory for me. We had one stop in Delhi on the way out to Australia with the sole purpose of going to see the Taj Mahal. My brother was not impressed with India in more ways than one, especially with the taxi drivers. The local train to the Taj from Delhi was not a pleasant experience for him; he found the poverty and smells nearly unbearable.

My brother survived India; I found it fascinating and yet at the same time distressing. The hustle and bustle of life, the contrast between the rich and the poor, and women arrayed in colorful saris all intrigued me. The street life was unlike anything I'd ever seen before; whether the destitute bodies lying on streets unattended were drunks or poverty stricken, I had no idea. People passed them by as though they didn't exist. India in those days had to be seen to be believed.

I already felt a connection with India since my grandmother had lived there for about thirty years. On my visits to her, I had sometimes opened the tin box of photos, old sepia-toned pictures of course, to look through the ones of my grandparents' years in India. In one, she was sitting side-saddle on a horse. Another photo was of my grandfather with a pith helmet and plus fours, as they were called in those days, trousers that went to below the knee with knee length socks—knee length socks in India in such heat! I have in my possession a photo of my mother at about three months old sitting on the lap of an Aiya (an Indian nanny).

We didn't stay long in Delhi, much to my brother's relief. We were met at Sydney airport by another one of my brother's friends, in whose home we were going to stay for a couple of days. This friend was Australian and had been in England for some time when my brother met him.

I remember going on a date with him when I was modeling, and he took me to the Playboy Club in London. I had five pounds and I decided to gamble on the roulette table. I just played the black and red, giving myself a 50/50 chance of winning. I seemed to guess right every time and soon gathered a crowd around me who were putting their chips on whichever color I placed my chips. They say the casino always wins. Not this time as I had the good sense to quit after my five pounds had made seventy sterling pounds. I had made one hundred pounds, but then my luck was starting to run out and I was placing my chips on the wrong color. I quit while I was ahead.

That was the first and last time I ever went to a casino and that was the only date I had with this guy. Just as well, since now he and his wife were inviting us to stay with them. His wife was from a wealthy family in England, and it was no surprise to me that their home was beautiful. They took us to a famous fish restaurant in Sydney harbor, and I thought to myself, no wonder people immigrate to this beautiful country, as little as I had seen of it up to that point.

After a couple of days with these friends, my brother rented a car and drove us on a scenic route north to New South Wales to a town called Lismore where our cousins lived. Grandmother had written to Bruce and Elsie so they were expecting us, and it was especially nice to be so welcomed into their humble home.

They were in their seventies, and soon after our arrival, we met their three sons. All three were married and had children. In the evening of our first night our distant cousins had arranged a BBQ along with all the wives and children. How faithful our grandmother had been to keep up this correspondence with her brother and then the wife of his eldest son for more than fifty years.

John, one of the sons, had a cattle farm and owned horses. What terrific fun my brother and I had riding horses and rounding up the cattle and driving them into the corral. Once we had the cattle in the corral and they were going through single file, we had to put a pipe, like a type of gun, down the side of each of the animal's mouths, squeeze a trigger, and shoot some liquid into each cattle's mouth, continually, while still sitting on our horses, until all the cattle had this medicine.

I felt like a real ranch hand and I loved every minute of it. When the dredging, as this procedure is called, was done, I was ready to take off and gallop and thankfully I didn't fall off. That was the last time I rode a horse.

At last, our two weeks stay in Australia was over and we were heading back to England via Hong Kong. We didn't do much in Hong Kong, just walked the streets, did some shopping, enjoyed some local food, and took some rest for the long flight home.

A Turning Point

12
RIO

I was twenty-seven years old in 1978 when I was scheduled to go on a flight to Rio de Janeiro, Brazil. The crew had two days to stay in the luxurious Sheraton Hotel. My hotel room not only overlooked the Copacabana beach, but I had a balcony as well. Standing on the balcony and looking out to the sea, I thought to myself, "Is this it, this kind of life?"

I've always loved swimming in the ocean and relaxing on the beach, so that is what I did for those two days in Rio. Late in the afternoon on the second day, I remember going out onto the balcony of my hotel room again and looking out at the ocean, watching people on the beach, just a mass of humanity, then coming inside to my beautiful hotel room.

Kneeling by the side of the queen-sized bed, I started to pray, "God, what is the matter with me? I earn a good salary doing a job I like; not many jobs take you around the world and vacationing on 90 percent discounted airline tickets. When not flying, I spend my time playing tennis at a sports club and do just what I want to do and at the end of the day, I'm not satisfied. There is no real purpose in my life. I can't justify my existence with a nice sun tan and by traveling to nice places. All I really want is for someone to love me." And right there in that beautiful hotel room, I began to weep in a heap on the floor.

13
AN OLD HOUSE

Soon after getting back to London from Rio, I had the opportunity to buy a small terraced house, which cost eleven thousand sterling pounds. I only had to put a thousand pounds down as a deposit, and then I obtained a grant from the council to put in a bathroom since the toilet was outside! I guess it was built before the First World War. I felt quite pleased with myself to have accomplished buying my own house, which I had to move into quite soon after I had the house papers, since my salary couldn't manage a mortgage and paying rent at the same time.

I recall so clearly getting into bed that first night, sitting up looking around—my clothes on a metal rack, the bare floorboards, dust everywhere—and thinking, "This isn't going to love me." I felt lonely and lost, and I started to cry.

When I wasn't on a trip, I was no longer playing tennis, but rather scraping paint off the mantelpiece, and I wasn't enjoying that one bit. Since my bathroom wasn't finished, I had to use the toilet outside even in the middle of the night! I wasn't exactly happy with the accomplishment of purchasing my little house.

A New
Relationship

14
A RELATIONSHIP

Soon after I had moved into my house, my old school friend, Jennifer, called me after not being in touch for a few years and asked me to go with her to a London theatre to see a well-known pop group live that night. I thought anything was better than scraping paint so I said, "Yes, I'd love to go. Where shall I meet you?"

She gave me the address, and when I asked whose house it was, she answered, "Dad's London house, I'll see you there at 6:00 p.m."

Before I had a chance to think of a place to meet other than her dad's house near Parliament Square, Jennifer had put the phone down. I was already starting to get nervous; at the same time an excitement rose up within me.

Thirteen years had lapsed since the incident when Alan had kissed me on the bed of that hotel room in the south of France. Part of me wanted to go and see him again just for curiosity, so I dressed up and drove myself to the address Jennifer had given me.

A butler, no less, answered the door, took my coat, and informed me, "Sir is waiting for you in the drawing room upstairs."

I mounted the staircase and arrived on the first floor of this beautiful townhouse not far from Big Ben. I entered the drawing room and there he was, a handsome man well into his fifties.

The first words out of his mouth were, "I've waited a long time for you to become a woman because I want to marry you."

I was stunned, just as I had been thirteen years ago, not because of a kiss this time, but by his words. Once again, I was extremely nervous that his daughter, my friend, was going to walk in on this scene as he was holding me close until I was able to release myself from his gentle hold. Within moments of Jennifer arriving, she said, "Are you ready then, shall we go?"

I thought to myself, "Yes, I'm very ready to go," and we were on our way to the live performance.

We sat in the front row, but I hardly took in the performers and loud music; my head was spinning, nearly out of control, due to what I had just experienced. All I could think was, *Danger, stay away.* I don't think in my whole life I have been more tempted to do something when all the while, I knew I was heading for nothing but trouble.

An interesting sentence in the Lord's Prayer is: "Lead us not into temptation!" Even though he was living in a townhouse in London, he still had a country house with a wife, and together they had three daughters. He told me he was separated and was getting a divorce. Did that make it right? No, even more reason to stay away, but I didn't. The following day he called me to take me to dinner. Every ounce in me told me to stop this and say "No" but in the weakness of my flesh I said "Yes."

As to be expected, an expensive chauffeur-driven car arrived at my door, and that was the beginning of the end. Once Alan took me on a dinner date, his daughter, Jennifer, knew what was in the making.

"You enjoy it while it lasts, but he will never marry you," she warned me. "I've seen this happen too many times in the past."

I took no notice and, somehow, she didn't mind me seeing her dad. If I wasn't dining at the Savoy Hotel in London, it was another restaurant of equal class and elegance. He adorned me with two different colored fox coats, a mink coat, and diamonds. He gave me a car, and we traveled in a limousine whenever we went to the theatre.

Jennifer couldn't convince me it wasn't going to work out, and it wasn't long before her father said to me, "Since we are going to get married, there is no need for you to continue flying for British Caledonian Airways."

He was already buying another flat in London for me to live in until we were to be married. He obviously didn't think much of my little two up, two down, a British way of saying a small house with two rooms upstairs and two rooms downstairs, and before long he had "his guys" in my house to finish renovating it.

Before I knew what had happened, he was taking over my life; I was being "swept off my feet," and I didn't mind one bit. He was kind and gentle all the time. I sold my house, making a profit of eight thousand pounds in less than two months. I moved into a London flat he had bought all decked out by a professional interior decorator. I had told him I couldn't bring myself to live with him until we were married, so having another address seemed the next best arrangement.

Meanwhile, I had given my notice to the airline at the end of May 1978. I invested the money I had made on my house in stocks and shares. Alan taught me to "play the stock market," so daily I looked in the newspapers to see if my shares were making money. Needless to say, I had half my money invested in his company.

Every day Alan would just give me money to spend. "Go down Bond Street and buy yourself clothes." He took me to Gucci, also on Bond Street, and bought me beautiful Italian clothes and accessories, which cost him hundreds of pounds. If Gucci wasn't enough, he bought me a burgundy-colored bag from Cartier. Alan was extremely generous, but then he could afford to be, since he was a millionaire. He made a lot of his money just talking over the phone, so we were together much of the time even though he had two offices, one in London.

He wanted to give me a dinner party in his smart London home for my friends. I invited my brother and his wife, my friends with whom I played tennis at the sports club where I was a member, and their husbands and boyfriends. Alan bought each of the ladies a Gucci key chain and had it on the placemat where they were to sit that evening. My sister-in-law still has hers, and in fact when I visit most of these girlfriends today, after forty years have passed, they still use their Gucci key chains; all but me.

We went to Ascot horse races, dinner and dancing in smart clubs in London, and even to Spain in his private jet. I loved being with him. We even traveled down to Somerset, a beautiful part of England, to look for a country house he wanted to buy for us. It seemed to me that nothing could be more perfect and nothing could go wrong. I thought I had never been happier.

What was Jennifer thinking all the while I was in a relationship with her father? Believe it or not, Jennifer didn't mind one bit, since she said that her father had never paid her so much attention since he was with me. She actually admitted that she had never seen her father happier than when he was with me. Nevertheless, she tried again and again to let me know that he would never marry me. Hers were words I didn't want to hear; I wanted to prove her wrong. Anyway, that was my thinking all the way through those never-to-be-forgotten nine months.

15
ABANDONED

The dreaded day came when he said, "I can't do this to you, I can't take your life away from you, I am much too old for you."

"You can't do this to me," I said, "You have already taken my life from me. I've left everything for you, sold my house, resigned from my job," and all the while, Jennifer's words were ringing in my ears. "Don't fool yourself, he will never marry you, you will end up hurt and one of his many girlfriends."

She was right; I was to become just one of his many girlfriends. But it wasn't quite over yet. He said he was going to Switzerland to have a medical checkup.

While he was gone, I called my girlfriend, Geraldine, and she and her husband came and moved me out of the flat I had been staying in those past nine months. When he returned, and found me gone with his photo turned down, he was furious, Jennifer told me later. As rich and as handsome as he was and as much as I believed I loved him, I thought, "I am not going to beg or grovel, I will just leave."

I took nothing of his or any of the many gifts he gave me, the fur coats or the diamond ring. I left everything in the apartment. I took the car for my convenience for the time being. I didn't want a constant reminder of him once we had parted. It was all too painful, and I didn't need to be reminded of what a fool I had made of myself, let alone the humiliation I felt.

At this time my grandmother, with whom I had always been close, was in the hospital. She was in her early nineties and frail, and she needed someone to live in her house. When I told her I needed a place to live, she was more than happy for me to live in her house since the only way she would be discharged from the hospital was if someone would stay with her.

Her house in Epsom, Surrey, was a far cry from where I had just come, but it was a home and a safe place for me to stay until I had my life back together again. Nana, as I called my grandmother, was fine at home during the day. It was just that her doctor didn't want her to stay alone at night. So, this was a good arrangement, since I was about to embark on a new career, or so I thought.

I remembered while I was still flying, being at the airport on standby in case another hostess did not check in for her flight. During that time, some other hostesses on standby were talking about a French cooking school. At that time, I was very happy flying around the world and was not in the least bit interested in being a cook. However, for some reason I took note of the address of the French cooking school they were talking about in Wimbledon, South London. So, remembering I had this number tucked away somewhere, and finding it, I called Mrs. Russell who ran the school.

I drove over to Wimbledon, found her residence, and talked with her. She said I was welcome to start a course of ten weeks the following Monday. Perfect timing, so I would have something to do and something with which to occupy my mind, which was still reeling from having been abandoned.

Recovering Again

16
COOKING SCHOOL

Monday morning came, and I found myself to be one of sixteen young women around a very large and long wooden table in Mrs. Russell's home kitchen. Her daughter taught the cooking classes alongside the aging Mrs. Russell, who sat and dictated recipes.

We all introduced ourselves, and I can't remember if she introduced herself or if Mrs. Russell introduced her, but there sitting at the kitchen table was Lady Diana Spencer.

I knew who she was immediately; Sarah Spencer was her older sister who was seen often enough in the newspapers with Prince Charles, who also happened to be seeing Camilla Bowles at the same time. Mrs. Russell had us pair off for our ten-week cooking course, and she paired me with Diana.

We became partners in the kitchen and cooked together for the next ten weeks. Whether we were cooking the entrée for the day, preparing vegetables, stirring a Béchamel sauce, or washing dishes, we did it together. Diana was ten years younger than my twenty-seven years. Nothing was further from any of our minds than that one day it was going to be Diana, not her sister or any other woman for that matter, who would be Prince Charles' bride. I wish I had a photo taken of us!

After Alan's return from Switzerland, it wasn't long before Jennifer told her dad where I was. He was soon knocking on my grandmother's front door. I would be lying if I said I wasn't glad to see him. He came upstairs to see where I was living and clearly wasn't impressed. He insisted on taking me to lunch. I should have told him to leave, but once again my heart was ruling my head and my good sense, so we were on our way to a restaurant.

I was quick to tell him I was doing a French cooking course, not wanting him to think I was pining away over him, and that Lady Diana was in the course as well, and we were partners in the kitchen. In fact, I went on to tell him that Diana had invited me to her mother's London flat on a day I had driven up to London for some reason.

It was near the time of Prince Charles' thirtieth birthday, and I asked her if I could see the invitation to the party at Buckingham Palace. She showed it to me, and she asked my opinion on which of two gowns to wear for the party. I remember saying, "Both are lovely, either one would be a good choice to wear."

I went on to tell Alan how much I was enjoying learning to cook French food. He had cooked for me and was an excellent cook. He told me how much he wanted to be with me, but he couldn't divorce his wife. Over lunch he told me he wanted me to keep the car he had given me and gave me back all the jewelry. He didn't argue about taking back the fur coats. They certainly would have been of no use to me in my new lifestyle, unless I sold them and gave the money to a good cause.

Alan drove me back to my grandmother's home in Epsom, and I thought I had finally seen him for the last time. However, it was not the last time; our paths would cross just one more time after an event that would change my life forever.

17

A NEW BEGINNING

I had lived with Nana for about two weeks when, on a Sunday morning, I went to her room to give her a cup of coffee. One glance at her and I knew she wasn't quite "with it." I don't know why I didn't call her doctor, but I didn't. Instead, I had this one thought: I have to get to church and pray for her. I hadn't prayed in a long time, not since wanting to be accepted by the airline. Without taking my handbag, I took the keys to my car and drove to an Anglican church not far from Nana's house. I went to that church because I had met the vicar, Derek Bedford, on several occasions when he visited my Nana and I had been visiting her on my way back from a flight.

I arrived at the church and turned the round, iron handle of the old wooden door and pushed it open. The service had started and a hymn was being sung, and I didn't think to pick up a hymnbook, so I just went and stood in a pew.

A lady in front of me turned around, smiled at me, and gave me her hymnbook, pointing to the hymn being sung. I returned her smile and appreciated her thoughtfulness. After the hymn was over, the congregation knelt and waited for a lady in the congregation to stand and say prayers.

In this Anglican Church, prayer was offered up to God for the queen, for those that rule, for tragic current affairs going on in the world, and then lastly, a prayer was offered for those who were sick and suffering in the parish. The lady praying named several ladies for whom to pray.

Among the list of names read was Edith Strowger, my grandmother. I looked up and my eyes glanced over the congregation; I thought to myself, "Are they really praying for Nana who is about to die?"

Yes, I really thought the end was near for Nana. I felt desperate and there above my head suspended from the ceiling was a bronze representation of Christ hanging on a cross. I couldn't take my eyes off of Jesus just hanging there. I remember as though it was yesterday looking at that cross thinking to myself, "I have lived a totally selfish life doing absolutely what I wanted to do, not giving much thought to anyone else but myself, and here people who perhaps don't even know Nana are praying for my grandmother who is dying," or so I thought. I had just come out of a relationship that left me at twenty-seven feeling as though I was in a pit; I was alone, wretched, abandoned, and humiliated. I had reached rock bottom.

I started to weep quietly and said, "Oh God, I am so sorry, please help me," over and over again. I guess I was just telling God how I felt and that I was truly sorry for what I had done. Did I really think God would hear me? I didn't know, but I kept saying I was sorry and, weeping, asked God to help me. Even if I thought He did hear me I never in a million years thought God would respond to my cry for help.

After the lady finished praying, another hymn was sung and the service was over. I never even heard the vicar's sermon or him telling us about Jesus. The vicar was surprised to see me as I left the church, and I told him I thought Nana was dying and he said he would come. Within a short while I was back with Nana. I went straight to her bedroom, and there she was sitting bolt upright.

She said, "Where have you been?" I realized she had had a "turn," and thankfully it had passed and now she was hungry and wanted her breakfast. I told her I had been to church. She responded, "Why?"

I told her, "I had a strong urge to go, so I went."

As I prepared her breakfast, I felt some change had occurred in me. Derek, the vicar, came to visit Nana and was glad to see her sitting up in bed, looking far from death. I inquired as to whether there were any other services during the week and he told me that on Tuesday morning there was a Holy Communion service at 7:30 a.m. I started to go to those services as well as the Sunday services.

I felt entitled to take Holy Communion because I had been confirmed at school when I was twelve years old. So, two days later, I was back in that church at the 7:30 a.m. service before going to my cooking class. I knew something had happened to me, and yet I couldn't explain what it was. I thought it had something to do with being in the church building. I knew I had always felt guilty about the sin in my life, and that was because I was guilty. I carried shame, and plenty of it, and guilt from the abortion I had (which was no less than murder). I had always lived under a burden that I was carrying, but now I felt different, as though the burden had been lifted from me.

After one Tuesday morning service, before I drove off to my cooking class, Derek suggested I join a Bible study. My immediate thought was, "Oh no, that's for old people" since that was true of that church, Christ Church. But not wanting to be rude, I told Derek that I knew which Bible study group I wanted to be in if I was to join one. (Typical of me, still thinking I knew best.) I described a lady in the choir to Derek and told him I wanted to be in the same group as her.

He said, "Jessica isn't in a Bible study group."

I said, "Then you put me in a group."

He had four Bible studies to choose from and he put me in Don Strickland's group. Don collected me from Nana's house the following Wednesday evening, and I told him, "Don't ask me anything because I don't know anything about the Bible."

He assured me he wouldn't ask me anything. We met at Hetty's house, a dear, sweet, elderly lady in her seventies, who lived in a council house. She had arranged her garden fold-up chairs to make enough seating for the eight or nine who were to gather in her little home that evening.

I sat waiting and thought, "If only my sports club friends could see me now with these folk!" The room filled up and I was thrilled to see the very lady with whom I had asked Derek to put me in a group. I came to know at the introductions that her name was Daphne (I had meant Daphne, but Derek thought I meant Jessica). It didn't take me long to get to know Daphne, a kind, godly woman. Daphne's good friend Elisabeth also attended the same Bible study and the two of them, in their fifties, took me "under their wing."

After a couple of Bible studies, Daphne and Elisabeth gave me a book called, *When the Spirit Comes* by Colin Urquhart. I had never read a Christian book. The evening they had given me this book, I heard one of the younger members of the Bible study group say, "With Jesus in my heart . . ." and I thought, "What is he talking about?"

I went home from the Bible study and started to read the book Daphne and Elisabeth had given me. In the first chapter I read words to this effect, "If you know what you have done is wrong and truly repent and ask God to forgive you, Jesus will give you a new heart."

Oh, my goodness, I didn't need to read any more to know that Jesus had given me a new heart. I didn't have to say, "Jesus, I want that new heart," he had already given it to me. That Sunday morning in church, quietly weeping my way through the end of the service, telling God I was sorry for sinning and asking for His help, was the beginning of a new life for me.

I was sincere that morning, and God knew my heart and that I was indeed truly sorry for the wrong I had done. Now I knew it wasn't being in the church building that changed my life. It was Jesus. I was only thinking about the recent relationship I had had, but that was a start, for God was going to then deal with all that guilt and shame I had carried over many, many years.

One of the first Bible verses I remember reading in the Bible study group was John 3:16: "For God so loved the world that He gave His only Son that whosoever believes in Him should not perish but have eternal life." There was no stopping me then; I started to devour books about Jesus, reading testimonies of how God had changed the lives of other people and how He wanted to use them to make known to others that He was indeed the Savior of the world.

I read the Gospels in the New Testament and read all about Jesus Christ—who He was and what He did and so much more. I loved going to church on Sundays as well as Tuesday mornings, and I could hardly wait for Wednesday night Bible study. I was reading that the Lord Jesus Christ was the One in whom to put our trust and hope, who told us He would never leave nor forsake us, and promised those who surrender to Him, "And surely I am with you always, to the very end of the age" (Matthew 28:20b).

Often, after arriving at Bible study, the husbands who worked in the city of London were talking about Dick Lucas and what he had preached that day during lunch hour in St. Helen's Church. I couldn't imagine businessmen in their pinstripe suits filing into a church every Tuesday and Wednesday over their lunch hour. Really, I couldn't fathom such a thing during the week. I was led to believe churchgoing was only for Sundays unless you were going to an early morning Holy Communion as I was doing on Tuesdays. I had so much to learn.

In fact, I was so enthralled with what they talked about and what they heard Dick Lucas preach that I decided to go into the city of London the following Wednesday to hear him for myself.

St. Helen's Church is a large church, and I wondered if many people went to hear him on a Sunday since his church was in the middle of London, in the business area. In I streamed, along with city men taking a half hour lunch in a church.

I'm a front row seat person, not wanting to be distracted by people in front of me. Exactly on time, Dick Lucas mounted the pulpit and announced a hymn. Once the hymn was sung, he started his message, which he spoke in just ten minutes and which I remember to this day, forty years later.

On that day so many years ago, he said words to this effect: "Do any one of you know of a person who is persecuting Christians and condoning murder in the church?"—no, I thought to myself—"Then if God can change the heart of Saul of Tarsus, who was that man, to become the Apostle Paul who wrote some of the letters in the New Testament and the book of Romans, then God can change anyone you and I are praying for."

That was all I remembered. But that was enough to make a lasting impression on me regarding praying for those who don't know Jesus. Even in that church, I was thinking of Alan and praying for him to come to know Jesus. Dick Lucas' message lasted ten minutes and then he ended in prayer.

At the back of the church a plowman's lunch of crusty bed, cheese, and soup was being served, as it was every Tuesday and Wednesday after the short service was over. This all took about half an hour from the first hymn to finishing a quick, healthy lunch to allow the second service to begin after all the businessmen and a few like me had left the church. We had not only fed our stomachs with the food, but I came away having been fed in my mind and heart with the word of God.

That evening at Bible study, I was able to interact with those who had also been at St. Helen's church and had heard Dick Lucas' lunchtime message.

A few weeks later, Elisabeth heard that Dick Lucas was going to be leading Bible studies in a country retreat center. We signed up to go. We were glad we hadn't missed that weekend to be stimulated and challenged by the Word of God.

Up until this time, I felt like I was always justifying my existence. I had always wanted to be liked for who I was, not for what people could get out of me. But now, I had found a group of people whom I really believed liked me for who I was. I loved being in their company and learning with them and from them all I could about my Father in heaven, His Son Jesus Christ, and the Holy Spirit. Just to think I could carry around in my heart the Spirit of God was amazing.

I was still living with Nana, and she was doing okay. Nana, however, thought I was going overboard with my new-found faith.

Every night, after I had said "good night" to Nana, I went to my room, knelt down at the end of my bed, lit a candle, put the lights out and said, "I'll go anywhere for You, Jesus, just tell me where You want me to go." I didn't expect to hear an audible voice, but I just kept telling Jesus, over and over again, "I'll go anywhere for You."

In Bible study, we had learned about King David in the Old Testament being a man after God's own heart. So along with asking God what He wanted to do with my life, I also said, "Lord, I know I don't deserve a husband, but if you have a husband for me, please give me a man after God's own heart."

My desire to marry was ever before me, but what was more important to me now was to surrender myself to Jesus Christ and do what He wanted me to do. I was starting to read books about people who had become followers of Jesus Christ and were serving Him in different parts of the world.

One of the first books I read was *Chasing the Dragon*, written by Jackie Pullinger, an English woman who boarded a boat in the 1970s and asked the Lord to tell her when to get off the boat. It docked in Hong Kong, and she felt led by the Holy Spirit that this was where she was to get off. The Lord led Jackie to the Walled City and she remained there ministering to drug addicts for the next forty years.

I saw her for the first time about four years ago in a large church in Los Angeles, and she still lives and works with drug addicts in Hong Kong. She married one such man whom the Lord delivered from drugs. Her story and a few other stories like hers impressed me so much that I kept praying and praying, "Lord Jesus, where do you want me to go?"

It was about six months of keeping this up and sitting in the dark with one candle on the floor at the end of my bed each night of the week, when India kept coming into my mind. Then during the day, I would pick up a magazine and see Mother Teresa on the front cover with an article inside. Was God speaking to me in this way?

I read another article of a major who was in India during World War II and later went back to India to feed two thousand homeless people every day. I even considered finding him to help him! I did write a letter to Mother Teresa, but, I was to be told a few years later, she never answered any letters because she was too busy caring for the destitute from the streets of Calcutta. These were the people she cared for, telling them about Jesus and giving them dignity until they passed away from this life.

I finally said, "Lord, what could I possibly do in India? I'm not a teacher or a qualified nurse. How can I see people with leprosy, let alone homeless children in the streets begging? But if this is your will for me to go to India, please give me the heart to go."

By this time, my cooking course was over and I had no interest in cooking director's lunches in London. But I did need a job while I was waiting for the Lord to tell me my next step in my newfound faith. A café on High Street was hiring a waitress in the town where Nana was living. I applied and got the job.

It was a far cry from the glamorous job in the airline, which it was in the seventies, but serving food and drinks all amounts to the same thing whether you do it in the air or on the ground.

My Bible study group was talking about going to the Albert Hall in London to hear Luis Palau, an evangelistic speaker, one Saturday afternoon. I volunteered to drive my car and about eight of us went. I had never been to a Christian evangelistic meeting, so I didn't really know what to expect. The Albert Hall could seat over five thousand people, and it was packed.

The meeting probably began with prayer—all I remember was those people in that hall were on their feet singing, "Our God Reigns." I was speechless. The sound was beautiful, and I thought to myself, "Where have I been all my life? Why didn't someone tell me about Jesus?" I'd never heard of Luis Palau, but when he started to give his message, he could have been talking directly to me, because he was talking about morality.

When the meeting was over, I told the people I had driven up with that afternoon that I was sorry, because I was not going to be able to drive them home. That was not a problem as they took the train home. I wanted to stay for the evening meeting and attend the same meeting all over again. I sang the same hymns, heard the same message, and could have stayed for a third meeting had there been one.

I came out of the meeting, and it was dark. Someone handed me a flyer, which I read as soon as I received it: "Spring Harvest, a Christian festival." The flyer mentioned a few names who were going to be the speakers, among them Stuart Briscoe and Francis Schaffer. I had no idea who any of these people were. But what I did think to myself was, "If these people on this bit of paper are anything like Luis Palau, then I am going." My Bible study group booked our accommodations, and we would be on our way to Spring Harvest a few weeks later.

I called my friend Jane, with whom I had gone to Spain on holiday and with whom I had modeled, soon after I knew I was a believer in Jesus, because I couldn't wait to tell her. I went up to London and arranged to meet her for lunch. I remember starting out, "Jane, I really don't know all that has happened to me, but I will tell you what I do know."

She listened with interest and was following me and at the end she said, "I want what you have." I told her the best I could, that it was a matter of admitting we are sinners, being truly sorry for our sins, acknowledging that Jesus went to the cross bearing our punishment of all that we have done that is wrong. The best part of all was that Jesus puts His Spirit in our hearts. Jane invited me to stay with her the following weekend. We went to a small church on Sunday. Monday morning I traveled back to Epsom.

I arrived at Epsom station to see the rain pouring down. It was an easy walk to my Nana's house, so I stood under cover until the rain stopped. While I was waiting, a young Asian woman stood beside me. I asked her where she was going and she told me she had an interview at the Manor Hospital, which I knew to be a mental hospital since I had volunteered a couple of times to go visit the patients there (was that ever depressing), as it was one of Christ Church's outreaches on Sunday afternoons.

I told her I would be glad to take her in my car, but first we had to walk to my grandmother's home and get my car. We put up our umbrellas and walked and talked together. Little did I know that that walk with Cecilia, a Malaysian girl, would begin a new direction in my life.

I asked her to tell me about herself and she said she was a Christian and had just come off a ship that traveled around the world with Christian literature on board. I told her I had just become a Christian, and I was excited to hear more of her story. She had been with an organization called Operation Mobilization and the ship was called Doulos, which in Greek means, "servant."

My new friend Cecilia asked me, now that I was a believer in Jesus, what I was doing. I told her I wasn't doing anything other than taking care of my grandmother and working a local job. I went on to tell her that I thought that Jesus wanted me to go to India.

"That's a big step for a new believer," she said. "I would like to invite you to the Operation Mobilization headquarters, where I am currently living in Bromley, Kent, so you can talk with some people there, as the organization has workers in India."

I thought this was a good idea, so the following Saturday I arranged to have lunch with Cecilia and others who worked in this organization, to talk with them about going to India. Meanwhile, we reached Nana's house, and I drove Cecilia to the hospital for her interview and waited for her to finish and took her back to the station, only to see and visit with her again the following Saturday.

My friend Geraldine hadn't heard from me in a while and called me to come and visit her. I went to her house to be told that Alan had invited her husband and us for dinner that night. My thought was, "If anyone needs Jesus, he does."

There was a bit of excitement about going because I felt I had a new "force" within me. He had bought another house near my friends and was there by himself. He was a good cook and made a delicious meal.

Little did Geraldine know that she was in the very early stages of pregnancy; she wanted to leave early after dinner because she felt nauseated. I remember having a vodka or two, and I wasn't ready to leave yet since I hadn't told Alan about Jesus. Alas, I never did get to tell him about Jesus, and the inevitable happened.

When Alan drove me back to Geraldine's house the next morning I told him about the gospel. I knew I had messed up, yet again, but still I told him that I had become a believer in Jesus Christ, and I had surrendered my life to Him. He said something like, "Yes, yes, I know all about that." Jennifer had told me that his mother was a devout Catholic.

There was nothing more to say. I got out of his car, said, "Goodbye" to him, and I never saw him again. Alan passed from this life several years ago.

I drove back to Epsom and got to work in time to open the café for breakfast. I did not feel physically well. I started up the grill, and before long, I was in the restroom throwing up. I have hardly ever had a hangover in my entire life, but I did that morning.

How could I have been so stupid as to drink the night before, especially knowing it was my one chance to be a testimony for Jesus? But no, I had to go to Alan's house thinking I had it all worked out and under control. I can just hear Jesus saying, "I guess I am going to teach this child of mine a lesson this evening that she can do nothing without me."

I thought I could resist Alan and stand on my own two feet and share the gospel. Now, looking back, I see that I didn't pray and ask the Lord to go before me and give me the words to say. Instead, I said to God, "Stand back, Jesus, and look what I'm going to do for You." What I did do was fall flat on my face, failing miserably.

After work I went to visit Elisabeth, one of my spiritual mothers who had given me my first Christian book. She had a friend staying with her from Guatemala. Her name was Agnes, and she was a believer. I recall telling Agnes what I had done the night before, because I couldn't tell Elisabeth, knowing I had disappointed her, God, and myself. I told Agnes, just having met her, that I had more than disappointed God; in fact, I had convinced myself that God wouldn't want me anymore if I could be so fickle in my new relationship with Him. I felt like "that was it;" I was done and would never be forgiven. I so clearly remember what she said, "See our life with the Lord Jesus as a battlefield. He actually has won the battle for us, but we are active soldiers and we are at war with the devil who wants nothing more than for us to go back to our miserable, old way of life. Now the truth is, you, Kelly, have fallen to the ground, but you are not dead, so for heaven's sake, get up and continue to fight the battle."

Those words spoke to me and that is exactly what I did. I repented; I confessed. I cried and told Jesus how sorry I was and asked Him to forgive me that I had failed Him. Because of what He did on the cross, dying for my sins, I knew He had forgiven me—again. "If we confess our sins, he is faithful and just and will forgive us our sins and purify us from all unrighteousness" 1 John 1:9.

Learning in Christ

18
A TRIP TO ISRAEL

I had been going to the Bible study for about three months when Elisabeth told me she was going on an organized trip to the Holy Land and someone in the group had dropped out—would I like to go?

"Yes, yes, yes," I told her; I would love to go with her to Israel. Up to this point I still had money, so I paid the tour company and was off to Israel with Elisabeth. It was a great trip and for the first time in my life I felt really, really happy. I was with Elisabeth, whom I had grown to love as a mother, and I enjoyed every moment of the tour, especially getting to know other believers on the trip.

As the tour guide talked about the events in the Bible, I was a bit lost since I didn't have much of an understanding of the Old Testament. Even though I don't remember all he told us, I remember all the places we visited: Bethlehem, Jerusalem, Bethany, Joppa, Gethsemane, and the Via Dolorosa, the path it is said that Jesus walked outside of the city gate to be crucified. I also remember taking a boat on the Sea of Galilee and floating in the Dead Sea. While on the shore of Galilee I told the Lord I never wanted to smoke another cigarette, and from that day to this, thirsty nine years ago, I haven't.

Our tour leader was a canon in the Anglican Church. While waiting to board the bus on one occasion he asked me, "What are you going to do when you get back to England?" I told him I didn't know but I wanted to understand the Bible.

"Why don't you go to Capernwray Bible School?"

I told him I didn't do well at school. He said, "It isn't like a regular school—there you can learn about the Bible."

Once on the bus, I turned to Elisabeth and told her I wanted to go. Her reply to me was, "Then all you need to do is get an application, fill it in, and send it off."

"Will you help me with the application, Elisabeth?"

"No, you can do it. If you are meant to go, God will see to it that you go," Elisabeth retorted.

Once home I wrote for the application. It really didn't ask much more than, "What is your testimony?"

Well, I knew that like the back of my hand and wrote it out just as I have written it in this book. Not long afterwards, I received a letter of acceptance to start at Capernwray Bible School on September 1, 1980, in Carnforth in Lancashire in the North of England.

But I am ahead of myself, and even though I had Bible school to look forward to, little did I know all that would transpire between coming home from Israel in March of 1980 and my first day at Bible school on September 1st.

19
A CHRISTIAN CONVENTION

I was glad to be back in Epsom with Nana (my mother and father went to stay with her while I was in Israel) and to continue meeting with my Bible study group. It was within a couple of weeks of arriving home from Israel that Spring Harvest Christian camp was to start.

It was around this time also that my Nana's doctor decided that she needed more round-the-clock care, and so she went into a nursing home. True, she didn't like it one bit, but her doctors said to me, "You have been with her nine months, and there is nothing more you can do for her here."

One afternoon when I had gone to see Geraldine, I had a strong urge to get back to Nana. It was good I listened to my feelings, or should I say leading of the Holy Spirit, because I found Nana on the floor when I reached home, and obviously she couldn't get up. After informing her doctor of this latest fall, it took about a month before Nana was settled in a nursing home.

I carpooled with friends from Bible study down to the south of England and got settled in our accommodation for the Spring Harvest Christian camp. The first evening there was worship and a message, but it was the following day's Bible study that I still remember.

The Bible teacher, Stuart Briscoe, was going to teach on 2 Peter in the New Testament for the next six mornings. He started every morning by saying, "So I will always remind you of these things, even though you know them and are firmly established in the truth you now have. I think it is right to refresh your memory. . ." (2 Peter 1:12, 13).

Well, I didn't know what Peter the apostle was talking about, so I wasn't being reminded; I was hearing for the first time.

That morning we were being taught from 2 Peter 1:16-17:

> For we [Peter, James, and John, three of Jesus' disciples] did not follow cleverly devised stories when we told you about the coming of our Lord Jesus Christ in power, but we were eyewitnesses of his majesty. He received honor and glory from God the Father when the voice came to him from the Majestic Glory, saying, "This is my Son, whom I love; with him I am well pleased."

There was another man by the name of Francis Schaeffer at this convention. He was an afternoon speaker, and the auditorium wasn't full. He was short, balding with thin gray hair and a goatee beard. What really made him stand out was that he was wearing plus fours, those knee-length trousers, and long socks. I wondered, "Whoever dresses like that in this day and age?" But, obviously, he did. He reminded me of my grandfather's pictures from when he lived in India. I sat alone quite some distance from the stage and I wondered what on earth this man was going to talk about.

He came to the front of the stage and said, "If you think that I don't know that maybe two-fifths or three-fifths of you women sitting in this Christian convention have had an abortion, then you are mistaken." I was shocked—how does this man know I've had an abortion? He went on, "I am not here to condemn you, only to let the world know what we are doing. If you know Jesus Christ as your Savior and have repented and asked Him to forgive you, believing He has taken this sin to the cross and died for you, then you are free and forgiven."

Francis Schaeffer talked about the horror of abortion because life begins at conception, not at birth. He said, "Who are we to decide who should live and who should die? Only God has that authority, not man." Dr. Koop, the US Surgeon General, was standing with him on the stage. Together, these two men had made a documentary called "Whatever Happened to the Human Race?"

Francis Schaeffer said much more, and as part of his presentation he showed the film. We saw an actual abortion being performed. Once the doctor had torn away the fetus from its mother's womb, it was simply thrown in a trash bucket in reach of the doctor. That is what I remember more than anything else.

Once the film ended I ran to my room, hoping no one was there, and fell to the floor and cried and cried. "Oh God, please, please forgive me for what I did. I murdered my own child." I had asked God to forgive me of this sin before, but seeing the operation and the fetus already in the shape of a baby with eyes, arms, and legs, knowing it had a heartbeat, brain, and organs forming, just being ripped out and then thrown away as garbage—it was terrible.

After some time, when I had gained some control of myself, I decided to go back to the auditorium and buy the book Schaeffer had recommended, *How Should We Then Live?*

On my way there, along a corridor, Francis Schaeffer was walking towards me. I looked at him, and he looked at me. It was as plain as could be I had been crying. He stopped; I stopped. He reached out his arm, and my face went into his shoulder. He didn't say anything and I didn't say a word either. It was probably just five seconds that I was still and standing with Francis Schaeffer, but I will never forget it as long as I live. It was this man and what I saw, an abortion being done, that caused me to know that human life begins at conception. Truly, God knows how sorry I was and still am for taking my own child's life.

There were several other speakers at Spring Harvest that week. One with whom I spoke after he had given a seminar was used by the Lord to confirm where I thought the Lord was leading me. After this man had shared his teaching I went up to him and told him I had heard Dick Lucas some weeks prior, and that I had been praying for a man with whom I had a few months earlier ended a relationship. He interrupted me and said, "Tell me about what God is doing in your life."

"I believe God is calling me to India."

"Really?" he said, "And how long have you known Jesus to be your Savior?"

"About nine months."

With raised eyebrows and another "Really?" he said, "That might be so, but I suggest you go to the mission exhibition hall and talk to people with Operation Mobilization who go to Europe for three months in the summer, to basically get your feet wet for overseas missions."

"Fine," I answered, "if you are suggesting that, I will go now and find someone to talk with about missionary service."

I met with a couple and they gave me some books to read and suggested I join OM's summer program. I had no plans until September 1st, when I was going to start Bible school, so the timing seemed good. I planned to go to Belgium for June, July, and August.

After this convention I wanted to be baptized. I had been christened as a baby, as I told you earlier in this story, but now I wanted to make my own public confession of giving my life to Jesus by immersion baptism. The Anglican Church I attended only had a font in the back, so that wasn't going to work for me. I knew there was a body of water in the Baptist church in Epsom, a church to which I had only been once, just out of curiosity, to see what it was like. A couple I knew going to Christ Church attended a Pentecostal church as well, and they talked to me about being Charismatic and introduced me to the Pentecostal pastor.

I was so busy going to all sorts of meetings of all sorts of denominations; I was a sponge soaking up all I could about how different denominations worshipped God. By now I had been in meetings when people spoke and sang in tongues and heard prophetic words spoken with interpretations. This was all above me, but I was interested to learn about such things. In the end, I asked the Pentecostal pastor to baptize me in the Baptist church by immersion even though I was attending an Anglican church.

When I heard of an evangelistic meeting in my area, I would go. I dropped everything, not that I had much to drop since my life now was consumed with anything to do with Jesus. At one such meeting, Colin Urquhart was the speaker. He wrote the first Christian book I had ever read, *When the Spirit Comes*, so I was eager to hear him in person.

For some time, I had been praying about the jewelry I still had and knew I would never wear again. I had money that I had made on my house invested as well as a lot of expensive clothes. By now I was absolutely convinced I wanted to dedicate my life to Jesus. I didn't want to keep a "storehouse" of money in case Jesus didn't work. I now believed that Jesus would provide for me if I surrendered all to Him and served Him faithfully.

After some worship and just before Colin Urquhart was about to speak, an amazing thing happened. He said, "Before I bring you a message this evening, I feel compelled to speak a word that God is putting in my mind. There is someone here who wants to sell everything they have of value and give away all that he or she has. The Lord says, 'Go ahead and give it all away.'"

I knew that word was for me. I was kind of in shock that this sort of thing actually happened, but I went to my knees and said, "Thank You, Jesus." Of course, I could have been wrong about giving all my money away, but I did it anyway and felt a freedom from the one who had abandoned me. I cut all ties from anything that would remind me of Alan.

I gave my money away to a specific cause, and I thought afterwards, most of the money was not mine anyway. I did not earn it; it was given to me. The few thousand pounds I made on my house was mine, I supposed, but it was renovated for me so that did not cost me anything either.

Becoming a Missionary

20
A SUMMER IN BELGIUM

Another chapter of my life was about to begin. In preparation for my trip, I was reading a book for orientation called *No Turning Back* by George Verwer. Around this time, I hurt my back, which was going to hinder me for the next twenty years. All I did was pick up something an elderly lady had dropped which rolled under a table at a church fête. I could hardly stand up. Yet I was able to get myself to a chiropractor a couple of days later and have several treatments before I was on my way to Belgium. I made a brief stop at the OM headquarters in Bromley, where three months before Cecilia had invited me to have lunch and meet leaders who could help me on my way to India.

I had only one gift left from Alan that I had to sell. I drove myself in it over to Bromley. I had already sold the car but asked the buyer to come and take it from the OM headquarters in Bromley, which he did. My journey was to begin without any trappings from Alan or any reminders of him.

My life was so full now that I hardly gave him a thought apart from praying for him, which I continued to do for many years along with praying for his wife, whom he went back to, their three young adult children, his previous wives, his other children, and not least of all Jennifer. I wanted them all to know Jesus.

I actually sent Alan's wife a testimony of someone who came to Christ. I just sent the book anonymously. Maybe it wasn't the wisest thing to do soon after I came to know Jesus as my Savior, but God knew I was deeply sorry for being in a relationship with her husband and wanted her to know she had a Savior and Lord who had died for her too. I had met her as a teenager on a couple of occasions.

I continued to visit girlfriends whom I had known from school, modeling, and flying days. When I told them that I had become a Christian, they more or less said, "Oh for heaven's sake, Kelly, we are all Christians." To which I replied, "We might know that Jesus was crucified and died for our sins, thinking we have done enough good to get into heaven, but when we have a heart understanding for what He did, then we are talking about a different kind of understanding of Jesus."

My friends thought this was all a phase I was going through and it wouldn't be long until I would get over it and get this religious nonsense out of my head. Little did they know it wasn't religious nonsense but a relationship with our heavenly Father. Now I was His child.

I remember that evening so well at the OM headquarters. After supper, a video was shown, "Peace Child," a movie about Don Richardson going to Papua New Guinea to make Jesus Christ known among a tribal people. I felt well on the way to living a missionary life. This was all I could think of doing now, desiring to know Jesus and to make Him known.

That first night I slept at the back of a church building in a sleeping bag. This was the first time I had ever slept in a sleeping bag on an air mattress on the floor! I never went camping as a child. So, there I was, lying on the floor in my sleeping bag, reviewing the past few months of my life; I could hardly believe all that had happened.

Sleep must have overtaken me, since I was awakened to get moving on our journey to Belgium in the early hours of the next morning. We took the ferry from Dover across the English Channel and arrived at the OM conference center that same day.

I loved being among so many people, a few hundred, in the auditorium singing praises to God. The founder of Operation Mobilization gave messages challenging us to go into the harvest fields, countries all over the world, and tell the Good News of Jesus Christ. I had been convinced that God had put India in my mind and believed God was giving me a heart for that nation. When I walked into the auditorium for the first time, I saw a huge display of India on the platform. It came to my mind, "This is how you, Kelly, are going to India: with this organization."

About eighteen months after that thought, I was on a plane to Karachi, Pakistan. From there I took a train north with other team members to Lahore. I had a few days in Lahore and then I was in the back of a van with others being driven to Delhi, India. Once again, I am ahead of myself.

That summer of 1980 I spent three months in Belgium, two months in outreach and one month at the OM headquarters in Belgium. At the conference among the hundreds there was a nice girl, but large, and I thought to myself, "I bet I'll be on a team with her." Not only was I on a team with her, I was to share a tent with her, pitched in a field with the only running water coming from a tap in a barn. Well, if I had never camped as a child, I was certainly making up for lost time during this month of staying in a field!

Being an adventurous person by nature, this was taking me to the other extreme of what I had been used to. It was kind of fun even though the tent was just big enough to fit three of us, one being this very large young woman who I predicted would be on the same team as I was. What didn't help was that it was cold and raining most nights and I had to crawl out of the tent to go to the toilet—well, actually, no toilet, just a field. I had plenty of choice of where to go! With all my clothes on I crawled back into my sleeping bag and tried to go back to sleep.

There were a couple of drawbacks during this first month in Belgium. First, it was the wettest month of the summer there. Second, we had a guy on our team, who was married but who did not bring his wife, and he was a pain. Why he ever joined the summer campaign, was beyond me. Maybe his wife wanted to get rid of him for a month. He didn't do his chores and was generally disagreeable and lazy.

This gave me a rude awakening to other Christians who showed no evidence of the fruit of the Spirit in their lives (the fruit of the Spirit being love, peace, joy, patience, kindness, gentleness, goodness, faithfulness, and self control - Galatians 5:22). I remember one of our main leaders at the conference said that the leadership was praying for our teams to have problems and difficulties. I thought this strange, but as I continued to learn and understand about having a relationship with Jesus, it meant that the more problems you have, the more you have to depend on and trust Him for the outcomes.

If that month had its problems, I couldn't believe I was in for another trying month. I was asked to lead the girl's part of a team for the following month. I was sitting in the auditorium, and those who were called out were to come to their team leaders. Maxine was called to come to my team, so I said, "Hi, Maxine," and she put her head in the air and ignored me. I was never good at conflict. I had so recently become a believer that I did not know how to resolve conflict and this one hadn't even started.

I found out the problem. Maxine had come from New York with a friend and wanted to be on the same team as her friend. Maxine's friend was assigned to go to Italy and Maxine was assigned to Belgium. This did not suit Maxine one bit.

During our month together, a member of the leadership team came to our team to check in with us. They asked us if they could be praying for anything or anyone in particular. I never mentioned

Maxine's name, but I said they could pray for one of the girls on our team (there were only three of us on the team along with about five guys). It was only too obvious that Maxine was not a happy lady and made my life especially difficult, to say the least.

The end of the month came, and we were back at the conference center. Apparently, a leader told Maxine that they had been praying for her on the team. Surmising that I had told them something, she came looking—more like "gunning"—for me. I was in a room sitting on my sleeping bag. It was a bare room with no beds, just personal belongings on the floor beside the sleeping bags. Thankfully, no one else was in the room when she found me and started in on me, "How dare you talk to other people about me!" On and on she went. She left the room slamming the door.

I had never encountered anyone like Maxine in my entire life, and she was supposed to be a Christian? I went to find somewhere to hide and cry. I ended up in an empty laboratory (our conference center was an old university building our organization rented for three months during the summer). I prayed and asked the Lord what I had done to deserve this kind of treatment from an African American girl nine years my junior.

As I stood and prayed, the thought came to my mind that in order for God to redeem us, someone had to die. That someone was Jesus. Romans 6:23 says, "For the wages of sin is death, but the gift of God is eternal life in Christ Jesus our Lord." It cost Jesus heavily, the physical pain and agony of carrying the sin of the world upon Himself, and worst of all, He cried out, "My God, my God, why have you forsaken me?" (Mark 15.34).

The thought continued to go further in my mind, and I realized that when God wants to draw people to Himself, oftentimes someone is going to get hurt. I also realized that I mistakenly thought that being in the boat with Jesus, all would be calm. Wrong, my boat then was nearly out of control or about to sink, and I wondered what on earth had gone wrong. Then the strangest thing happened.

Maxine came looking for me and could have knocked me down with a feather by what she said: "No one has ever loved me the way you have loved me this past month and I want to thank you even though I have been nothing but a pain to you," and then she hugged me. Wow, she did surprise me. I kept in touch with Maxine for a few years after she went back to New York and then we lost touch. I will especially look for Maxine in heaven and listen to the rest of her earthly journey and where the Lord took her in life.

At the beginning of the third month, the same leader who said the leadership team was praying for problems and difficulties on the teams said, "We here at the headquarters are in a predicament. We are short of someone to work in housekeeping. Would anyone be willing to volunteer?"

My hand bolted right up in the air and, thankfully, it was the only hand that was raised, and so I was acknowledged to be that volunteer. Right after the conference I was in the laundry room, knee deep in mechanics' dirty overalls. The headquarters was the base for all the vehicles, vans, and trucks going overseas for the long-term teams heading out after the summer program.

When I was eleven years old and in boarding school, my first job during the holidays was helping out at our local launderette. Only then did I start doing our family wash in the machines. I was reminded of that experience when I found myself using these commercial washing machines. I sometimes stood among the dirty, greasy overalls and thought back to when I was with Alan, going to fancy restaurants, flying in his private jet, but really being in bondage. Here I was free, washed in the blood of Jesus, regenerated and redeemed, valued and loved. It was tough in one sense, but not in another, because I was meeting believers all the time and being a part of something so much bigger than anything I could have ever imagined.

The second week I was assigned to the kitchen and staff dining room. The chief accountant asked me at a coffee break, "Well, what do you do here?"

"Oh, I'm just working in the kitchen and dining room," I said in answer to his question. But what he said next I've never forgotten.

"You mean you work in the kitchen and dining room?"

"Yes, that is exactly what I mean, I am serving you in the kitchen and dining room," I said, leaving out the word, "just."

He made me feel my job was important. Sometimes I meet young mothers who say, "I'm just a housewife." My immediate response to them is, "You mean you are a housewife and home with your children; that is to be commended."

That chief accountant was not married. He volunteered for OM for years—thirty-seven, if I am not mistaken. He was impeccably dressed, and yet his office was his home. He lived and worked in his office. He called it a simple lifestyle.

I met some wonderful people that summer, a summer never to forget. In some ways, I thought it was my boot camp for missions. I knew God would not love me any less had I decided mission service was not for me. But I never wavered; I had started on my road to make Jesus known overseas, and I wasn't about to give up now even though I knew the road ahead was going to be difficult. I believed the Lord confirmed in my mind and heart that I would go to India with this organization, but not before I went back to England to attend Bible School for a year.

21
BIBLE SCHOOL

It was sad to see my grandmother on my return from Belgium. She did not like being in the elderly people's home and made that perfectly clear to anyone who visited her. I also visited my parents and saw that no change had occurred in their home or their hearts. In one of my father's sober moments he said to me, "You are a very lucky girl." I told him my life now was not about luck but about putting my hope and trust in the Person of Jesus Christ. Unfortunately the conversation stopped there. My mother continued to drink whiskey watching the television while my father was out buying rounds of drinks for "hangers on" at the pubs. But before my mother had "one too many" I would talk with her about Jesus; only in the end she would say, "Darling, I've been praying many more years than you, so you believe what you want to believe and I'll believe what I believe," and she did.

September 1980 saw me at Victoria Station in London to find the bus going to Capernwray Bible School in Carnforth, Lancashire. I sat next to a twenty-year-old American guy on the coach who told me he was going steady with a girl back in America. He was a nice young man who certainly didn't mind sitting next to a sister in Christ a lot older than himself. He had come to London by himself and as yet had not met any of the other students going to Capernwray.

Capernwray Bible School was an old converted castle. It had lots of character and a great deal of the interior was kept very much in line with the building. On arrival, I was shown to my room, which I shared with three other young women. We were a Canadian, an Irish, a Scottish wee lass, and me—I say "Scottish wee lass" because she was not much more than four feet in height. She had a rare condition whereby her bones didn't grow properly. But that wasn't all, she had multiple medical issues and had had numerous surgeries and was in pain most of the time. But she was going to put all that behind her for this year to enjoy studying the Bible.

When she dropped something, she couldn't bend and pick it up, so if I was nearby, I would pick it up and think no more of it—until one day she asked me to go for a ride in her little red car. Her car had been configured for her specific physical needs. We stopped where there was a nice view and she switched off the engine. She faced me and told me she had never lived away from home and her mother had always looked after her.

Glynis said, "If I don't make it this year living on my own, I never will. When I drop something, please don't come running to my aid; I have a hook on the end of a stick and I can manage to pick up what I drop. But there is one thing I need you to do for me, and that is, shampoo my hair. I can't raise my arms up high enough to do that."

I told her I would be glad to wash her hair whenever she wanted me to. We chatted and enjoyed the view until it was time to leave and head back to the castle. We were close friends for the next thirty-five years until last year when Glynis died and went to her eternal home, where she had longed to go for many years.

The first Friday night after dinner we were told to go to the auditorium for the principal, Billy Strachen, to give us some orientation. He was very humorous and had us in fits of laughter. The students liked him. He made one point clear, "Whichever seat you choose on Monday morning will be your seat for the rest of the semester." That was basically all I can remember him telling us, besides some funny jokes.

Students started to get to know one another over the weekend. Come Monday morning before breakfast, I walked to the front of the auditorium and along the first set of desks all the way to the middle of the front row and put my pen and notebook right in front of the podium. "Lord, if you don't teach me, no one will."

I loved all the classes, especially "The Person and Work of the Holy Spirit," which Billy Strachen taught. My understanding of the Old Testament was very limited, so taking the class on an overview of the Old Testament was especially interesting for me. There were so many other classes on the patriarchs, prophets, poetic books, and the history books, as well as John's gospel, the Letters and Revelation in the New Testament. I just longed for every day to start, so I could be there, sitting and listening to the speaker to learn what the Bible taught.

I recalled the time when my father had said there was no more money to send me to school at the age of fifteen and there in the bathroom said to myself, "One day I will take myself back to school . . ." And here I was fourteen years later back at school and loving it. "Thank You, Jesus."

Out of two hundred students, most were around the ages of eighteen to twenty-five, but there were about twenty of us in our late twenties or early thirties. One staff member with whom I really became friends was the dean of students. One day she asked me if I would host a couple coming from Columbia Bible College, now called Columbia International University, in South Carolina, USA. I told her I would be delighted to take care of them. The husband was the college dean of students. The purpose of their visit was to see if any credits from Capernwray Bible School could be transferred to CBC (as it was called then).

During the week in which they stayed with us at Capernwray, the dean of Columbia Bible School asked me what I was going to do after the year at Capernwray. I told him I was going to India for two years, but also that I wanted to know more about the Bible.

Right then and there he said to me, "If you ever want to come to Columbia Bible College, all you have to do is to get in touch with me."

There have been a few times in my life when I was sure, as sure as I could possibly be, of something; going to Columbia Bible College was one of them. I really liked this couple and we stayed in touch after they returned to the States from their week's visit to Capernwray.

I used to get up early in the morning long before breakfast and take walks. This castle was surrounded by farmland where sheep were raised. Having only ever lived in built-up areas, being in the countryside was sheer heaven.

I remember one morning I was a long way from the castle and I heard the fire alarm go off. Oh no, I thought, I was so far away that my only hope of getting in line to be counted was to run across the fields instead of keeping to the paths.

It had rained the night before and the ground was wet, so running across the fields was taking a big risk, but what else to do? So I started running to where I could see the student body, all 199 of them, lining up to be counted. As they were looking out in front of them wondering who was running towards them, the ground beneath me was soggy, and I went face down in the mud! I limped into line not knowing whether to laugh or cry. I must have looked a sight, and the students didn't know whether to laugh or feel sorry for me. Either way, it really didn't matter.

On one of those early morning walks I recall saying to the Lord, "Father, you know how much I love being here; could I stay and join the staff when the school year is over?" I have never heard the voice of God, but as clear as any words ever spoken to me, the thought came into my mind, "I know you love Me and I'll not love you any less if you stay here, but I have so much more for you if you step out in faith and go to India." I never again thought to stay longer than my one year at Capernwray Bible School.

22
INDIA

Two days before I was to leave for Belgium, I watched on television the Royal Wedding of Prince Charles and Lady Diana Spencer on July 29, 1981. Diana was given the title 'Her Royal Highness Princess of Wales.' I remember being on the floor in my sleeping bag at the back of a church thinking about Diana when we were at cooking school together and now she was on the Royal Yacht on her honeymoon. What a stark difference our lives had taken since those few weeks in Mrs. Russell's kitchen. My one thought was, "God, I would rather be here lying on the floor embarking on a lifetime adventure with You, Kings of kings, than to be the future queen of England and not know You. I don't envy Diana's life one bit."

Back in Belgium in August 1981 at the conference center I spoke with the women's leaders for those hoping to go to India. I was open and honest with them that I had only been a believer for three years and told them I had been working since I was fifteen and didn't have a degree or a qualification.

I wondered how being a model and a flight attendant would play into the equation of being a missionary as I interviewed to go to India. I admitted I wasn't a trained nurse or a teacher and I really did wonder what I could do until they asked me, "Do you drive?"

"Oh yes, I drive and have driven since I was seventeen."

I felt pleased with myself; there was something I could do that might see me on my way to India. What they didn't tell me was that I would be expected to drive a van in India—a large van at that. The many girls' evangelistic teams going door to door in cities of India needed a foreigner on each team to drive a van with the team's kitchen equipment, bedding, personal belongings, and the team themselves from one city to another every three months. But even with this qualification the leaders were still very hesitant to allow me to go to India.

"Kelly, how do you think you will feel on a team of seventeen- or eighteen-year-olds who really have not had a lot of schooling and certainly not had the jobs, the experiences, and the life that you have had and with one of them being your team leader?"

I really didn't think it would be a problem so they decided to take a chance with me. I'm so glad they did. Before leaving Belgium, I was given tire-changing training and other tips to maintain my van once I was in India, like making sure the radiator didn't overheat, which in fact did happen on more than a few occasions on long distance journeys.

I only had one mishap in nine months while I drove in North India. I skidded onto the other side of the road and ended up off the road. Thankfully nothing was coming in the opposite direction.

Once I was accepted to go to India I was on my way in just a few weeks. I was to leave in November 1981. As I mentioned earlier, I flew into Pakistan with others. The guys drove my van and a truck into Delhi.

One of the most important aspects of this journey to the subcontinent was a friend I made along the way. I met Gaynor from Wales at the conference a couple of months prior to our leaving. Our friendship began as we flew to Karachi, Pakistan, went by train from Karachi to Lahore in the north, and spent three or four days there. We traveled in the back of the van from Lahore to Delhi. After two or three days in Delhi, Gaynor had to leave with her van and drive down with others to the south of India. That was the beginning of a relationship I have had with Gaynor these past thirty-six years.

The first city I spent some time in was Varanasi, also known as Banaras on the Ganges, the most well known river in India. My first morning of outreach was in a Catholic Jesuit School. We had a book table there, selling storybooks about Jesus.

The city was dirty—trash in the streets, bicycles galore, street kids picking through garbage, dogs and cows in the roads—and there were temples everywhere, simply a mass of humanity.

If God had whispered in my ear that day that in thirteen years I would be living in this city of Varanasi for five years I would never have believed Him. It is a good thing God only reveals to us what we need to know at any given time.

Another very significant incident for me during those early months in north India in the state of Uttar Pradesh was when one of the women's leaders, who had interviewed me in Belgium, came to visit our team (now in the city of Allahabad) to find out how we were all doing.

She caught me on a bad day. It was that time of month and I didn't feel too great. Before I went out door-to-door that morning, she said, "Kelly, meet me on the roof after lunch and we will have some time together." I hasten to add that old Indian houses have flat roofs!

Cheryl, my leader, couldn't have picked a worse day to talk with me, or so I thought. After lunch, I climbed the steps to the roof where Cheryl was already sitting on the concrete waiting for me. I still had the stench of urine in my nostrils from the morning outreach where there had been some open sewers.

"So how is it going, Kelly?"

I managed to get out, "Okay, I guess," before the tears started rolling down my cheeks.

"What's going on?"

"Oh Cheryl, I came out to India to tell Indian women about Jesus, but I don't even speak Hindi and the girls with me just say to women who open their doors to us, 'Would you like to buy a storybook?' I think to myself, we have more than storybooks; we have forgiveness for our sins to tell them about."

I continued to say, "Yes, yes, I know I have come here to India to be an encouragement to these young girls who know little else than that they know Jesus as their Savior and Lord and that they are going to heaven."

Then I paused long enough for Cheryl to say to me, "Kelly, God has brought you to India to do a deeper work in your own life. There is really very little you can do for these girls, least of all for God. Do you really think God needs you? No, He doesn't. He can do everything very well without us or anyone else for that matter. Jesus only wants our hearts and for us to be surrendered to Him. The Lord Jesus wants to use us so we can share in the blessings of what He is doing in peoples' lives."

Those words were just what I needed to hear. From that talk with Cheryl, I had a whole new perspective on being in India.

The vehicle I drove had to go out of India every six months. The vans and trucks in India either had to be driven to Pakistan or Nepal. I had to drive my van to Nepal, which I did on three occasions. It was while driving my van to Nepal that another new friendship began to last the next thirty-six years. I met Hilary in Lucknow, a city in North India in Uttar Pradesh and the two of us drove from there to Kathmandu, by ourselves! We weren't sure of each other at first, but having no one else to interact with we began a great friendship. There are few people in my life that I can laugh and laugh with, but Hilary was one of those people.

Once my van was safely in the mechanic shop in Nepal, another van had to be driven back into India. That van was in Hilary's name. Driving to and from India and Nepal were some of my funniest memories. Back in the eighties, we had to cross one river before there was a bridge built. We had to drive our van onto a raft, and a Nepali with some kind of long pole, would help glide us to the land on the other side. I had done this a couple of times by driving onto the planks and up on to the raft. But one time a foreign guy who was in our company said he would drive my van onto the raft. I told him I could do it, but he insisted. I can only imagine that he wished he hadn't insisted, because he drove my van off the planks and the van ended up suspended over the water!

In India, there is something you can count on, and that is, when an accident happens a crowd will gather, not in minutes but in seconds. Thankfully, enough men gathered around to pick up the van and put it back on the planks for me to drive onto the raft. Needless to say, we all laughed at this hilarious incident. It wouldn't have been funny if someone had been hurt, but thankfully no one was. Those were the days!

Engagement

23
A BIBLE TEACHER

By April of 1982 I had been in India just a little more than four months. All the OM Indian teams were to come together for Bible teaching in the city of Gorakhpur, in the state of Uttar Pradesh, close to the Nepal border. The seminar was going to be on the first letter of John.

Periodically, since committing my life to Jesus three years prior to this time, I had continued to pray, "Lord, if you have a husband for me, I only want a man after your own heart, and if you do have someone for me, Lord, please drop him right in front of my face because I know myself; I will forever be looking left and right thinking, could he be the one, or that one?"

My first love was the Lord and nothing and no one was going to come between Jesus and me. Realistically, at the age of thirty-one, the chance of meeting anyone in India was pretty slim since there were very few foreigners with our organization in India and most of them were younger than I was. So, here I was with a group of students attending the Bible seminar, and we were waiting for the teacher to appear.

About thirty Indian guys were seated on one side of the room and about the same number of Indian girls were on the other side. Additionally, about three foreign girls and three foreign guys were attending the seminar, including myself. I was sitting at the back of this classroom—unusual for me, as I usually take the unpopular seat in the front row. The classroom was outdoors but with a roof. I was looking forward to this study.

As the study of 1 John got underway, I was impressed with the instructor and his teaching. In fact, I thought he was an excellent Bible teacher. Why I thought he was single, I don't know; but he was. He was 6'2", good looking, and about my age. The thought did come to my mind, "Could I marry you?!" Where did that thought come from!

The next class I was sitting in the front row, not because of the teacher, but because his teaching was so good I didn't want to miss a word he was saying. I interacted with team members, but only the girls, since in those days, talking to the Indian young men was culturally inappropriate. As the study went on for a couple of days, I thought that the teacher was a bit standoffish as I never saw him talk to anyone or even saw him around. In fact, he was in his room preparing for the next class.

This was his first time teaching the Bible to OM teams after having been on a men's team in Bihar, in north India, mainly in the back of a truck or driving from village to village listening to the Indians on his team preach the gospel of Jesus Christ through a loud speaker and distributing gospel literature. The leadership had taken note that he had Bible teaching gifts, which proved to be right.

I continued to be impressed with his teaching. In one of his classes he told us that if he was honest he preferred spending time reading books rather than interacting with people. My immediate reaction was, "Really, I couldn't imagine anyone wanting to be with books more than people. There is no way you and I could have a chance of being together." Then I began to notice his clothing and shoes. "Trousers are a bit short, and as for those shoes, they are awful." I guess I was convincing myself that there was nothing right about him but his teaching.

At the end of the study the teacher gave us an exam, and I thought I had done quite well. The last question was: Write a definition of justification. I thought I had answered the question adequately—but not according to the teacher, which will come to light later.

The week seminar was over and our girls' team spent another three months in another city, Jhansi. While in this city in May 1982, I received a telegram that my grandmother had passed away. She was ninety-nine years old when she died. It was a sad time for me. But I pressed on, as I had to drive to the foothills of the Himalayan Mountains to a city called Mussoorie for another week-long seminar on the book of Romans. The same teacher who taught us the first letter of John three months before was assigned as the Bible teacher.

For some reason, I didn't sit in the front row for his teaching. After he had taught on Romans 10, I went up to him and spoke to him on the last part of verse 14: "And how can they hear without someone preaching to them."

"With that being true," I said, "it isn't the only way God speaks to individuals."

It was important to me to say that this was not the only way that people encountered God—our God did not need to use humans to make Himself known.

I told him in about three minutes flat about my first repentant encounter with God—that I had messed up, gone on my knees, told God I was sorry, and asked Him to help me. He heard me, and from that moment on, my life was never the same.

I continued that no one had pointed their finger at me saying "You are a sinner" and told me I needed to repent and accept Jesus Christ as my Savior. I later learned how this impacted my teacher, who had seen me around and surmised that I was superficial.

There was another Bible teacher at this conference, a pastor from Britain. I had talked with him, and he had complimented me to the Romans teacher, who by then had been traveling around

India teaching and beginning to think it would be better if he were married.

Just as I had said, "Lord, if you have someone for me, I want a man after your own heart," he was saying to the Lord, "God, if you want me to be married, You bring the woman of your choice into my life."

After he had heard what the British pastor had said about me, the teacher was bothered with me on his mind. "Oh no, Lord, no, not her, she is way too sanguine for me, too outgoing and friendly!" But apparently, I got stuck in his head and on his heart, and I wouldn't budge from bugging him!

A few months later we had an All Indian Conference at the same place I attended my first seminar in Gorakhpur. The US director of OM asked me if he could have a word with me, and I wondered, "Why would he want to talk with me since I am under the British leadership?" He told me, "Someone is praying for you."

Now in this organization in India back in the 80s, young men and women were not free to make their own acquaintances or "hang out" to get to know each other. No, if a guy liked a girl he had to discuss it with his country leader and have him approach the girl he liked and get her thoughts on the guy. So, I asked, "Who is it?" to which he replied, "Roy Clayner."

I didn't give myself time to think or even say, "Oh, I have to pray about this." No, not me, I just shot a quick response.

"Absolutely no, he would rather keep company with books than people, according to him. We couldn't be farther apart than chalk and cheese."

"Then you will have to write to him and tell him you are not interested."

"Okay, I will." And I did. I wrote and told him I thought he was an excellent Bible teacher, but as far as he and I having a relationship, I couldn't see it in a million years.

He received my letter just before he had to return to the States, since he was an American and had to leave the country every six months. Apparently, he was pretty sure that the Lord had put me on his heart, and talked to his parents and a few friends about me. Once a girl turned a guy down in this organization that was supposed to be the end of it and the subject was closed. His country leader, however, suggested he write to me again. This he did.

Back in July in Mussoorie, I had been asked to be the girls' team leader at the headquarters in Bombay (as it was still called in those days). Although I went to Bombay after the All Indian Conference, it wasn't what I really wanted do. I wanted to stay on an evangelistic team in north India as a team member. My job now was to lead a team of girls who worked in the headquarters office. I was not warmly welcomed by some of these girls, all of whom were Indians except two. I had been asked to come from "outside" when one Indian girl on the team in particular thought she should have been asked to lead the team. I wasn't liked by that girl, and she made it perfectly clear to me that she was not going to cooperate with me. Not a pleasant situation to be in, but there was little I could do about it other than to do my job.

Another aspect of my job or ministry at the headquarters was to look after sick team members that came in from the field and take them to the hospital if necessary. Also, I had to purchase the dry stores, tea, coffee, rice, etc. for the team house, numbering about forty people, which was a big headache, as I had to balance the accounts. Figures were never my strength, and this responsibility was one I didn't like.

It was January 1983, and some new foreigners were arriving from the UK; I wanted to make them feel welcome and help them get settled in before most of them went out into teams across India. One such person was Sue Halstead. She was to become one of my closest friends for the next thirty-four years. Six years after I met her, Sue founded Love in Action, a ministry that rescues girls who have been kidnapped or sold into prostitution. In the past thirty years, about one thousand girls have stayed in the home she started, and nearly all have surrendered their lives to Jesus to be their Savior. A book, *A Hand From Heaven,* was written about Love in Action a few years ago.

Sue was a nurse and was excellent with figures. I couldn't have been happier when the leaders decided to keep Sue at the headquarters with me. Sue could have led the team standing on her head she was so capable, but unfortunately that assignment had been given to me.

Ironically enough, after Sue arrived we seemed to get an influx of sick team members coming to the base with typhoid and many other illnesses. Without Sue's medical knowledge, I would have been in over my head. I needed help, and the Lord sent Sue just at the right time. I couldn't have been more grateful to God.

One Saturday morning I went to my mailbox and found a letter from the US, which seemed quite bulky. I recognized the writing immediately. "He" wrote to me, and he was not supposed to, according to the rules. I went out in the garden, settled myself on a bench, and opened the envelope. I began to read the four-page airmail letter from Roy, the Bible teacher, in which he candidly shared, even in the first paragraph, that he believed the Lord had laid me on his heart and thought that one day I might consider being his wife.

He also shared his life story of leaving college in his third year and heading out to India; he wanted to test his faith and prove Jesus to be all that Jesus said about Himself. He told me in his letter that he had resisted me at first because I was so outgoing, knowing he was an introvert. He kindly mentioned that even though I had written a terrible definition of justification (on my exam), it was not a good enough reason not to pursue me!

I shared this letter with Sue first of all. I asked her what she thought. Sue responded, "It doesn't matter what I think, what do you think?"

I visited a friend whose husband was in leadership and she said to me, "Do you want to know what Eric thinks?"

"No, Mary, I don't, but you are going to tell me anyway, so get it over with."

"Eric thinks you are an absolute fool to turn Roy down."

I didn't admit to Mary that what her husband had said made me stop and think. Was I a fool to turn Roy down? I also asked my friend Hilary her opinion, and she kindly gave it to me. "Kelly, you are thirty-one years old, for heaven's sake, just talk to him!"

I thought that was good advice! No harm in talking with him since he was due back in India soon and was coming into Bombay for a few days. I thought it was going to be a bit awkward, since I was in charge of hospitality and he would stay in the guest room. But it was another friend who really spoke into my heart about Roy.

I took Jill out on a boat by the Gateway of India in Bombay and told her about Roy. Interestingly, she didn't give me any response or opinion. Jill was visiting us and considering joining our organization in India.

After dinner, Jill called me into her room and said she had been praying about what I had told her while out on the boat that afternoon. She said a verse kept coming to her mind.

"It doesn't mean anything to me but perhaps it will to you." She read me the verse from the Old Testament, 1 Samuel 16:7.

> But the LORD said to Samuel, "Do not consider his appearance or his height, for I have rejected him. The LORD does not look at the things people look at. People look at the outward appearance, but the Lord looks at the heart."

This was the first time I had heard the answer to a prophetic prayer.

All Jill had done was to ask the Lord if He had something to say to me, and she waited all afternoon until He gave her the verse above. Meanwhile, I had been busy asking my friends what they thought instead of going to my heavenly Father and asking Him what He thought. Jill's words hit me like a thunderbolt. I had been bothered by his trousers being too short and his shoes, while all the time our Lord is concerned with our hearts, not our clothes or shoes. Regarding the bookish person that he was, Roy was going to be so beneficial to me later as he helped me grow in my love and understanding of Jesus through the books he suggested I read. Authors like Martin Lloyd Jones and J.C. Ryle to name just two.

I went to my leader and asked if I could meet with Roy once he arrived back in Bombay, because I'd changed my mind and decided I did want to meet him. The request was granted and it was arranged that we meet one afternoon at Café Naz on Malabar Hill. Roy was already there when I arrived. We were soon in conversation, and it was one of those times when I believed the Lord impressed upon my mind something He was saying to me. "This is the man I have for you."

Even with His confirmation, I still thought, "Lord, if this is the man You have for me, You better make it work, because apart from You, Jesus, I don't see that we have a thing in common."

By July 1983, four months after that first meeting, we were engaged in Bombay, a few days before I left India to return to England. Roy was fine to marry me that summer, but I told him I couldn't, because I had been given an invitation by the dean of students at Columbia Bible College in South Carolina on the east coast of America, and I wanted to go study there for one semester. Roy supported my desire to do more study of the Bible and said he would go back to India while I was in the US.

24
MY MOTHER

On my return to England in August 1983, I wrote to the dean of students asking if I could come to Columbia Bible College from January to June, 1984. I submitted an application, and on it, I must have included that I had never finished high school, but somehow, I was accepted to go for just six months.

This gave me some weeks to spend with my church family and spiritual mothers, Daphne and Elisabeth, as well as my own family.

I took my mother out for a picnic and told her about Roy. I asked about her wishes regarding my wedding the following August and her reply was, "Darling, you can do just what you like because I won't live long enough to see you married."

I thought my mother would be delighted, but instead she predicted her own death. Not the nicest thing a daughter wants to hear when she is going to be married. I thought about getting married in Pennsylvania where Roy's family was from, but I thought no matter what my relationship was with my parents, which was pretty nonexistent, they were my parents and I wanted to honor them. Now that I knew the grace of God in my life I thought it was the least I could do to see them happy for me on my wedding day. As it turned out, my wedding day did not turn out at all how I was hoping it would, but that was still a year away.

I recall two very sad visits with my mother after coming home from India. She had been drinking and said she wanted to bring out the Ouija board. I was shocked that she even had a Ouija board. She turned a wine glass upside down and told me to put my finger on the glass. All I did was pray, "Jesus, take charge here." My mother couldn't understand why the glass was not moving about the board. She said, "It always moves," and I said, "Well, not today." And she put the board away.

Sometime after this incident, I visited her again and she told me she needed Elisabeth, my spiritual mother. I told her she didn't need Elisabeth, she needed who Elisabeth had living inside her, Jesus.

"Mother, you can ask Jesus into your life right now. You, or anyone else for that matter, can't get good enough for God. All you can do is confess that you are a sinner and that you have sinned against God, acknowledge that Jesus died on the cross for you personally, and ask Him to forgive you, and He will, if you are sincere. You don't need me but if you would like me to pray with you to receive Jesus Christ as your Savior and Lord, I will."

"Yes, I want you to do that for me."

So, I did and just before my mother was going to acknowledge Jesus as the One who died for her sins, she said, "I can't."

I asked her, "Why not?" and she said, "My guides won't let me."

My mother had given her allegiance to Spiritualism for as long as I can remember. If only I had known then what I knew years later, I would have commanded the evil spirits (two guides) to come out of her in Jesus' Name. This saddened me deeply, knowing she was possessed by evil spirits. At times, she never seemed to be herself.

1 Peter chapter 5 verse 8 says: "Be alert and of sober mind. Your enemy the devil prowls around like a roaring lion looking for someone to devour."

25
BIBLE COLLEGE
IN THE USA

Roy came from India in November and met my parents. They felt very awkward meeting him, knowing he was a Bible teacher. Roy had been brought up in a home where alcohol had never been consumed.

Roy only met my mother that once, and even then it was only for a few minutes. I felt sad that on that day when I introduced Roy, soon to be her son-in-law, she didn't even offer him a chair with the intention of sitting with him to get to know him. Little did I know at that time she was very sick.

We spent Christmas that year with my brother and his wife, a time when they were happy to get to know the man I was going to marry. I was to leave soon after Christmas for South Carolina to attend Columbia Bible College. Since I was only going for six months, I wanted to study by auditing classes so I would not have the pressure that comes with exams or writing papers. I knew I couldn't pass exams, and I had never written a paper. That just scared me. But God had other plans for me.

I arrived at the college and went to stay with the dean and his wife, who lived on campus, for the weekend. They welcomed me graciously but told me some very sad news on my arrival. Their son had graduated six months earlier and had married his classmate and sweetheart. Only a few weeks prior to my arrival, both their son and daughter-in-law were in a car accident and died. Their only comfort was that their son and daughter-in-law were with Jesus, knowing Him to be their Savior and Lord.

My friend shared that the worst part was, none of the students came to visit, because they just didn't know what to say. For her, that was the whole point, "I didn't want them to say anything. It was I who wanted to talk to them about my son and daughter-in-law." I learned from her that when friends of mine lose a loved one I must intentionally go be with them—not to talk, but to sit and listen to them talk as much as they want to about their loved one and help them grieve in that way. So, my weekend with them was sober but good.

Monday morning saw me in my dorm room getting to know the girl who was to be my roommate. After breakfast, I was scheduled to see the academic dean who was assigned to all foreign students. His first question to me was what classes I wanted to take.

The first word out of my mouth was "Audit! I want to audit Romans, missions, family life, psychology, and take a couple of electives." He informed me that I was not allowed to audit classes. I had to take all my classes for credit.

I told him I didn't want to take the classes for credit because I hadn't come for a college degree, only to listen in class for one semester. He explained that because I had a visa to study in the US, I had to take classes for credit. Well, if the floor could have opened up, I wanted to be swallowed up right then and there. I knew I wouldn't be able to pass exams or write papers.

"Lord, why didn't you let me know I would have to take credits if I came to study at CBC?"

The thought came to me, "You wouldn't have come, that is why, and you are going to stop saying you can't do it. Yes, you can, because I am here to help you." And as the Lord said, so He did. I didn't get A's, but for me to get two Cs and one B and, dare I say, a D was good, and I was pleased with my effort and achievement.

Other students helped me with my papers, with how to use the library, where to find the information I was looking for, and how to do a bibliography. I recall hearing a student questioning a professor about why she didn't get an A+ when all I could think was, "Can't you be satisfied with an A?"

I mention this as some of us have been put down so much in life that we begin to believe we can't do anything and will never amount to much. I learned this is not true; those are lies from Satan, and there is no reason to believe them.

Western Civilization was one class that all new students had to take. While interesting, it had way too much information for me to absorb for the exam. Instead, I went for a long walk on the day I was to take that exam. No one said anything to me for not being present. A few days later I was on a plane back to England.

Apart from the classes I took, I enjoyed chapel every weekday morning more than anything else. Two chapel speakers stand out in my memory. Susan Baker sang "When I See Him Face to Face," which left not one dry eye in the auditorium. Susan was blind.

I had lunch with her in the cafeteria that day. She was from England. Susan had recorded some beautiful music, and I took some of her tapes with me back to India a year after I married. I actually sent one to Princess Diana when her marriage was in shreds. The words Susan sang seemed to fit Diana's situation at the time. Diana's secretary wrote and thanked me for the music I had sent Princess Diana.

Another visiting chapel speaker was Helen Roseveare. Helen was also English and worked in the Democratic Republic of Congo as a medical doctor. She tells in her book *Living Sacrifice* of how she was raped by Red Army rebels. It wasn't until she went back to England—primarily to take care of her aging mother, but also to eventually become a renowned speaker—that God revealed to her why she went through such horror in Africa.

When she spoke at meetings, women who had themselves been raped wanted to talk with her because they knew Helen had been through the horror they had been through and could speak into their lives.

I try to be very careful not to say, "I know how you feel" to anyone if I have not even the slightest idea what they have been through or are going through. But Helen's courage to share her story helped many women, as she understood what they had experienced and she pointed them to a Healer who knew all about their horrific plight. It is these kinds of people who are my heroes—those who live for the good of others, who have lived a life so worth living.

After one quarter, we had spring break, and another student was driving up to Pennsylvania where Roy's family lived. Roy's parents had invited me to visit and spend spring break with them. So with an invitation from the student driving to Pennsylvania, three other students and I took to the road and began our spring break.

Morris, Roy's brother, met me in Lancaster and took me to his parents. Roy's parents who had been in education, had retired. Roy's mom had been a high school English teacher and, after having her three children, was a second grade teacher for twenty years. His dad had been a high school guidance counselor. They retired before coming to England for our wedding. They were delighted to have me spend a week with them, so they could get to know me. I met Morris' wife, Lesley, on that visit, along with their four-month-old son.

Before I left to go back to Columbia, Lesley sat on the guest bed with me and said, "You are going to be very good for this family." I was overjoyed to hear something so encouraging and to be welcomed into my future husband's family while Roy was halfway around the world in India.

I thoroughly enjoyed my time at Columbia Bible College, but I reckoned six months was enough for me in that academic environment, and I was ready to get married. During this time, while Roy was back in India, we wrote many, many letters to each other via snail mail, since we didn't have computers in those days. I still have all of those letters and fully intend to read every one of them again one day, in my old age!

Marriage

26
A DEATH AND A WEDDING

Once back in England I had three weeks until I was to be married. Roy arrived from India one week before our wedding. Eight days before our marriage, I was trying on my wedding dress for alterations when I had a phone call from Elisabeth, my spiritual mother, "Kelly, your mother is in Epsom General Hospital. She is in a coma with a brain hemorrhage."

I walked into the ward and saw about five other beds in it, and there was mother by the window. She lay on her left side in a coma. There was no IV and no machines around her to keep her alive.

"You were right, mother, you aren't going to live long enough to see me married."

I was told that she had fallen down the stairs at home. I had my Bible with me and started to read some Psalms. Psalms are our emotions that we express to God. I had a lot of emotions that night as I sat with her. I prayed for her and talked to her. Did I think she could hear me? I didn't know, but I kept talking to her and reading from the Bible.

There was a time when I recall saying to her, "Mummy, if you can hear me I am going to tell you again about Jesus. None of us can get good enough to go to heaven. The Bible tells us that God loved us so much that he sent Jesus Christ into the world to die for us that we might go be with Jesus for all eternity as we acknowledge Him to be our Lord and Savior. Mummy, we can never save ourselves. All Jesus is asking of us is to repent and believe in His Name. Once we acknowledge that Jesus died for us, amazingly enough He sends His Holy Spirit into our hearts so we are never alone.

"Jesus said before He ascended into heaven, 'I am with you always, even to the end of the age.' Mummy, His words are true. Jesus has never left me one day since I acknowledged Him to be my sin bearer, my Savior. He has been with me every moment of every day for these past six years. Jesus gives us His peace.

"He says in John 14:25–27, 'All this I have spoken while still with you. But the Advocate, the Holy Spirit, whom the Father will send in my name, will teach you all things and will remind you of everything I have said to you. Peace I leave with you; my peace I give you. I do not give to you as the world gives. Do not let your hearts be troubled and do not be afraid.'"

Thick bloody jelly was coming from my mother's mouth. I went to find a nurse to attend to my mother. It was late in the night; other patients were sleeping, and all seemed relatively quiet. When I found the nurse she snapped, "Do you think your mother is the only patient in this ward?" This was the harsh response I got.

In my surprise, I responded, "No, so if you wouldn't mind giving me the disposable pads, I will change the pads myself."

I had obviously interrupted the nurse's break time, and she wasn't about to be disturbed. It didn't matter to me, since this was my mother whom I wanted to attend to in the last hours of her life. She was dying.

I honestly thought she would live another day. She was very overweight and had been for years. I guess I thought her body fat would just keep her alive a bit longer.

After spending a long night with my mother, I was getting tired. By 5:00 a.m. the nurses were starting their rounds. I stayed long enough to watch them man-handle my mother as they turned her on her other side.

The peace I had had that last night with my mother was now being taken away, and I thought it was time to leave. I went back to Elisabeth's house and as I got into bed, my father called me to tell me, "Mother has died." She was only sixty-nine years old.

I rang her doctor after some sleep, and he said, "Kelly, I wouldn't have given your mother another three months. She was a very sick woman. She had cirrhosis of the liver."

It was really the alcohol that killed her; never a day went by when I didn't see her drinking whiskey in large measures. Her life was a sad one. I know she loved me, though we had a bit of a love-hate relationship. When I left home at seventeen, she said, "If you leave this house, take everything with you and don't ever expect to use this house as a hotel." She didn't really mean that because she never wanted me to go. What mother in her right mind would say such words to a daughter she loved so much? I knew her words were a threat.

After her death I did something I regretted. I went to see her in her casket. She looked ghostly and not like my mother at all.

Three days before my wedding, Roy's parents, his brother Morris, Morris' wife Lesley, and their nine-month-old son, along with Roy's sister and a friend of hers arrived at London Heathrow from Harrisburg, Pennsylvania. On their arrival, I had to tell them my mother had died and her cremation would be the next day. They kindly attended my mother's funeral. It was indeed a sad occasion. There was hardly anyone there because my mother didn't have any friends. Two days later I was married.

August 4, 1984 arrived, and I had prayed and prayed it wouldn't rain. I was the one paying for my own wedding, and I didn't have money to spend on a tent. Alas, it rained. Our prayers are answered, but sometimes not always in the way we hope they will be.

My father and I were in a car driving to the church. He complained he needed a drink. Anyone who knows anything about alcoholics knows they end up with a bloated stomach and red-veined face; he was a sick man.

The best part of the whole day was our wedding ceremony. Roy was wonderfully supportive throughout all the drama around us. In England in those days, the bride's family took care of all expenses, but my parents didn't offer or have any money to give me a nice wedding. So instead of having the reception outside under a tent, it ended up being in a dismal, dark church hall.

A girlfriend who was also an air hostess had become a chef and had her own catering business. As a wedding gift, she kindly gave me the wedding reception food.

I had booked an excellent photographer, but an acquaintance said he would take the photos for free. I cancelled the professional photographer for the amateur, which turned out to be a big mistake. He apologized that the flash on his camera wasn't working on the day of my wedding. The photos were a big disappointment.

But one thing does bear mentioning, which really was extremely significant. Roy and I were with an organization that believed in the power of prayer and when they heard my mother had died a few days before we were to be married, they prayed for us.

In spite of the growing list of disappointments, I sensed that I was being "carried along" by prayer. The Bible tells us in Isaiah 40:28–31,

> Do you not know? Have you not heard? The LORD
> is the everlasting God, the Creator of the ends of
> the earth. He will not grow tired or weary, and
> his understanding no one can fathom. He gives
> strength to the weary and increases the power of
> the weak. Even youths grow tired and weary, and
> young men stumble and fall; but those who hope

in the LORD will renew their strength. They will
soar on wings like eagles; they will run and not
grow weary, they will walk and not be faint.

Had I not gone through such hardship during those difficult
days, I would never have experienced the Holy Spirit's presence
as I did at that time. I was tired, weary, and weak. But God gave
me strength and His power to come through those difficult days
by the prayers of those who knew me. There were even some who
didn't know me and who still gave their time to pray for me.

27
A YEAR IN AMERICA

After a honeymoon in Scotland, Roy and I flew to Philadelphia to spend our first year of marriage in Pennsylvania. Roy was studying to be an ordained minister and he needed a measure of understanding of Greek and Hebrew. We rented a small, old mobile home for six months.

During that time, I heard that Francis Schaeffer had gone to be with the Lord. I wrote to his wife, and told her how her husband, through the film he made with Dr. Koop, had helped bring healing and forgiveness into my life after I'd had an abortion. How kind of her to write me a reply. I still have her letter.

While Roy took classes, I volunteered at a crisis pregnancy agency. I could say to these mostly young girls who found themselves pregnant, "I know how you feel and understand your desperate situation. But you need to know exactly what you are doing before you make this life-changing decision to abort your baby."

We showed a video of an abortion; a baby being taken from a mother's womb. When these young girls saw the form of the baby being murdered and thrown in the bucket, they would often change their minds, carry their babies for nine months, and arrange for their babies to be adopted or fostered if they knew they couldn't take care of them. I admired these young women.

The second half of our year in America was spent near Roy's family. I was so welcomed by them and so happy to be a part of a peaceful and stable family. This was such a contrast from the home in which I was raised. I felt accepted and loved by his parents as their new daughter-in-law.

Primarily, we were getting ready to return to India, and Roy continued to study. During this year, I wrote a few letters to my father, knowing he would have felt the loss of my mother. I often wondered how he was getting along without his "Iri," as he used to call her, though her name was Iris. I also knew, judging by how awful he looked at my wedding, that he wasn't going to live much longer either.

28
ANOTHER DEATH

My brother met us on our arrival at London Heathrow airport. As soon as we were out of the parking lot and driving away he said, "Dad is in the hospital dying of cancer. I don't want you to tell him he has cancer."

He continued to tell us that the funeral home had contacted him because our father had not paid our mother's funeral bills. Faced with our father's irresponsibility once again, my brother was furious. My brother paid all of our mother's funeral bills and decided he was done with our father. But after some weeks he was a bit worried, knowing our father was not well.

He called our father several times but there was no answer. Instinct, or whatever my brother was feeling as an adult child of alcoholics, caused him to drive to our father's apartment. Although there was no answer to the doorbell, my brother thought he was inside. He broke the lock on the front door and forced it open to find our father painfully thin and in a near unconscious state. He later told me that our father's fingernails and toenails were disgustingly long, and while waiting for an ambulance, he cut them.

Dirty clothes and underwear were stashed in cupboards, and piles of unopened bills and mail were on the dining room table along with my unopened letters. Dishes in the sink had gotten the better of him, and he could no longer manage even to cook for himself.

Thankfully, my brother had reached him in time before his cancer and cirrhosis had completely destroyed him alone in the apartment. I had been in the States a year and I returned to hear that my father was dying.

On the day I arrived in England, I went to visit my father in the hospital. I asked Roy if he wouldn't mind if I went to see my father by myself. He wanted me to do what I thought was best.

Roy stayed with my brother at his home. My father was taken to a National Health Hospital and was in a ward with about eleven men. I was told which ward he was in, but I didn't see him when I first walked through it. I had to turn around and walk back down the ward, looking at each patient a second time, until I stopped and stood at the end of one bed looking at the man I thought was my father. He seemed nearly unrecognizable.

"Is that you, Kelly?"

"Yes, it's me."

"Do you know I'm dying of cancer?"

"Yes, I know you are dying of cancer."

"I don't want to die and I'm not ready to die."

Beholding my father in a pitiful state, suffering, I spoke the only words of comfort and truth I knew.

"Daddy, if I was in that bed instead of you, I wouldn't want to die either. I've only been married a year and I would love children, but if I was to die now, I'm ready." My father looked at me blankly.

"I know my Savior Jesus Christ died for my sin. He has forgiven me and set me free from all my guilt and shame. I have acknowledged Jesus as my Savior, and I am His child. He has imparted His Holy Spirit into my heart so that I know He is always with me."

I shared with my father what Jesus told his disciples in John chapter 14 verses 1-3 , before he was crucified:

> Do not let your hearts be troubled. You believe
> in God; believe also in me. My Father's house has
> many rooms; if that were not so, would I have

told you that I am going there to prepare a place
for you? And if I go and prepare a place for you,
I will come back and take you to be with me that
you also may be where I am.

"In John chapter 14 verse 6, Jesus said, 'I am the way and the truth and the life. No one comes to the Father except through Me.'

"Knowing this truth, Daddy, we can be ready to meet our Savior, but first we must confess our unworthiness, sins, and sinfulness and trust in Jesus."

After telling my father about salvation in Jesus he never said another word.

I should have offered to pray for him, but I didn't. I collected his dirty washing and planned to bring clean clothes back the following day. That wasn't going to be necessary.

My brother and I had a call the following day at 7:00 a.m.— he had passed away in the night.

"Passed away to where?" I wondered.

Eternity is where we all pass into; but into which eternity did he pass? I struggled with the thought. Was it an eternity with Jesus where there is neither abuse nor abandonment, no more tears or emotional pain, no more whiskey or drugs to deaden one's pain of living, or was it an eternity without Jesus? For me, hell would be a place where Jesus is not there.

My father was cremated at the same place where my mother was, with hardly anyone there, apart from Roy, my brother, and myself, as well as David and Penny, who also came to my mother's funeral.

My father, like my mother, killed himself with an excessive amount of alcohol and by smoking sixty cigarettes a day. A scripture came to my mind after my father's death. Jesus could have taken center stage and been crucified by Himself but He wasn't.

Instead he was executed between two men who, in contrast, were receiving due punishment for their crimes.

In the Gospel of Luke, chapter 23, verses 39 to 43, we are told,

> One of the criminals who hung there hurled insults at Jesus: "Aren't you the Messiah? Save yourself and us!" But the other criminal rebuked him. "Don't you fear God, he said, "since you are under the same sentence? We are punished justly, for we are getting what our deeds deserve. But this man has done nothing wrong." Then he said, "Jesus, remember me when you come into your kingdom." Jesus answered him, "Truly I tell you today you will be with me in paradise."

My understanding is that the one criminal had a repentant heart, and Jesus saw through his crimes and guilt and passed judgment on him right there on the cross during their final moments: not guilty.

Did my father consider what I had told him about Jesus? Did he ask for forgiveness from Jesus before he slipped away into eternity? I hope so, but I'll not know the answer until Jesus comes to take me home, to the eternal home He has prepared for me.

Children

29
BACK IN ASIA

Roy and I were on our way back to India soon after the death of my father. During our brief courtship, we had talked about having our own children. I was thirty-three when we married, and I had been surprised when we started courting that Roy was a little more than four years younger. We did not anticipate problems having children, so we waited a year before trying to conceive. But no baby came.

I kept telling Roy, "I believe God is going to give us two children, a boy and a girl."

I kept this up until one day he said to me, "Kelly, God has not spoken to you like He did to Abraham, when God told Abraham that his wife, Sarah, at the age of ninety years old, was going to have a son."

"True," I agreed with him on that point.

It wasn't long after we settled in the state of Gujarat in the northwest of India that we decided we should have some tests done to see if there was any reason why I was not getting pregnant.

I went to Bombay and saw a gynecologist. She did a small operation and found that my fallopian tubes were infected and blocked; without her trying to unblock them, I would never get pregnant.

She told me the cause of my blocked tubes was the abortion I had had eleven years before. After she did the procedure, I would have to wait one month before going back to her to find out whether the operation was successful or not. Waiting that month was agony for me.

In my quiet times, it was as though the Lord was saying to me, "Now who is first in your life, the desire for a baby or Me?"

In my anguish, I prayed, "You are, Lord, but if I will never have a child, please give me the grace to live my life without having a child or children."

During these days, I thought back to the abortion I had had. I was well aware now that life began at conception and that I had allowed a doctor to sever my baby from my womb. I told myself, "This is the consequence of that sin in my life." I knew God had forgiven me in Christ; I had specifically confessed the wrongdoing of deciding that my baby was not going to live. But now, because of that wrong decision, I might never have a child, and there was no one to blame but myself. I put the longing of a child "on the altar" every day that month.

I returned to Bombay at the end of the month. A friend, who remains to this day a dear sister in Christ thirty-five years later, accompanied me. The doctor injected me with a dye and did an ultrasound and turned the monitor towards me for me to see the dye flowing freely through my tubes. I couldn't hold back my tears. Joy filled my heart.

"I'm happy for you," said the doctor, "It isn't always success-ful, but it has been for you." I expected to get pregnant the next month, but I didn't. Nor did I get pregnant the following month or the month after that.

Before long, a year had passed and I had not the slightest hint of a pregnancy, even though the same doctor had given me fertility drugs towards the end of that year.

Roy and I accepted an invitation to join an evangelistic ship for six months with the same organization we were with in India. Roy was asked to be a conference speaker and I was assigned to work at the information desk. It wasn't long after joining the ship that I ran out of my fertility drugs.

I took an appointment to see the ship's doctor to ask him to renew my prescription. He told me he wouldn't do it. Roy and I went to see the ship's director, who was a friend and also a medical doctor. He said that when we docked in Singapore he would refer us to a gynecologist who had delivered one of his sons. Meanwhile, we were docked in Malaysia.

Not only was Roy a conference speaker on the ship but he also preached on Sunday mornings along with many other ship personnel at various local churches. One Sunday morning, Roy and I, as well as two other young women from the ship, were ready waiting on the quay at 7:00 a.m. for the driver to pick us up and take us to the church we had been assigned to that morning. That particular morning the rain poured down.

The driver eventually showed up in a small van. Roy sat in front with the driver, while the three of us ladies were in the back. I was sitting in the middle seat.

It wasn't long before we were on a dual highway, two lanes on either side of the median. For some reason, I felt we were going too fast on that wet road. Before I knew it, we were skidding, and moments later we crashed. Up ahead of our vehicle to the left of us had been a huge truck, and I knew our brakes had failed. We had lost control and collided into the back of that vehicle.

On impact Roy and the driver were unconscious. The windshield shattered, and the two of them were covered in blood.

Thankfully I was all right. I was able to slide the back door open and climb over an Italian girl whose knee was hurt. I made it over the median and saw a fire station in the distance. There were no cell phones in those days, so I ran to the station as fast as I could and asked them to call an ambulance.

When I got back to the scene of the accident, the emergency responders were already there. The paramedics were getting Roy and the driver out of the van and into the ambulance. I climbed in and sat on a jump seat facing them, as they lay stretched out on either side of me, still unconscious. This was the first time I had looked down at my white dress, now splattered in blood.

On arrival at the hospital we were rushed into Emergency. I didn't have the phone number for the church we were supposed to attend, so I called the ship personnel from the hospital and told them we had been in a road accident and we wouldn't make the church meeting.

I stayed with Roy waiting for him to "come to," and that only happened when a doctor was removing a piece of the windshield from his head.

I had told the ship personnel earlier that we had had a car accident that morning, and even though we were in the hospital, I said we were okay. They showed up around 4:00 in the afternoon to take us back to the ship, and they said, "If we had known it was this serious, we would have come immediately."

Since Roy was not in a life-threatening condition, I didn't want to make more of the accident than it was—interesting how we see and measure events differently.

With only a sore head and a few cuts and stitches, Roy was to take rest the next few days. The other two girls had minor injuries. Not so with the driver. He came off the worst, but I did see him before we left the hospital and thankfully he was fully conscious and being treated for his wounds.

I loved being out at sea. I guess it reminded me of being back at my boarding school in Eastbourne in Sussex in the south of England, lying awake at night, listening to the waves.

This was not a cruise ship with deck chairs lining the decks, so I went and bought myself a fold up chair and kept it up on deck behind the book exhibition at the stern of the ship. I sat here in the early mornings having quiet times with Jesus and gazing out at sea.

After Malaysia, our next port was Singapore. On our first morning there, Roy and I went to see the gynecologist to whom our ship director had referred us. I gave him my history.

"Have you ever been pregnant before?"—a question I hated being asked because I had to admit I had.

"Then we better do a small operation and see if you have endometriosis, which is a hard lining of the uterus wall that does not allow your egg to imbed easily."

I was admitted to the hospital and scheduled to have this procedure under general anesthesia. When it was over and I had come out of the anesthesia, the doctor came to see me.

Bracing myself, I sought the truth, "Please give it to me straight doctor if you see any reason why I cannot get pregnant."

"Mrs. Clayner, I see no reason why you cannot get pregnant. I did a D&C, a scraping of the womb to test for endometriosis, which you do not have; I took a cyst off one of your ovaries, and I brought your uterus forward since it was slanting backwards, which might be a reason why you are not getting pregnant."

I couldn't have been happier to hear this news. I stayed in the hospital just one night and then recuperated in an apartment that had been arranged for me for a couple of days, before returning to the ship, which was now in East Malaysia.

An English friend stayed with me in the apartment. The day after I came out of the hospital Rose said, "Let's go sightseeing!" I felt a bit weak but thought I could manage going somewhere by taxi.

"Taxi? No need to waste money on taxis, we'll get the bus," my friend said.

Without making a fuss I climbed on buses going to see the sights of Singapore with many sit-downs at each place. We arrived back at the apartment having enjoyed our day out, but oh, I was exhausted. My pad was soaked with blood; but what did I expect? I had just had surgery.

Rose offered to make me a cup of tea. Taking tea in the afternoon had always been my habit, but strangely enough that afternoon, I just did not feel like drinking tea.

The following day Rose and I caught a short flight to East Malaysia to join the ship. I was to start my shift at the information desk as soon as possible. I knew I couldn't sit at the information desk for a full eight hours keeping alert, answering phone calls, and making announcements, so I went to see Sherri, my supervisor, and admitted that I felt extremely tired and couldn't do my eight hour shifts.

"So what could you do?" Sherri asked kindly.

"I could mend the engineers' torn overalls if I'm given a sewing machine."

"Fine, I'll see to it that you get a machine and you can work when you feel the energy to do so."

One morning, not long after I started mending overalls, I was in our cabin in the tiny bathroom and I heaved as though I was going to throw up.

"Roy, I think I'm pregnant."

"Don't be silly sweetheart; you can't be. You haven't been back long enough since your operation."

I too knew it seemed impossible, but nevertheless I took a urine sample, hoping upon hope that a pregnancy test would prove positive. As soon as I knew the ship's doctor was in his clinic, I went to see him. I told him I thought I was pregnant. I also told him that I had been in the hospital and had a D&C (which is also done to abort a baby) a month ago. He said it would be too early to tell, but for some reason gave me an internal examination.

"Did you take a urine sample this morning?"

"Yes, I did."

"Go get it."

After the sample was tested and found positive the doctor said, "I knew you were pregnant because your uterus is the size of a ten-week baby."

"No, no, I can't be ten weeks since I had a D&C, which would have taken my baby from my uterus."

"I'm telling you, you are at least ten weeks pregnant, and when we dock in Bangkok I want you to have a sonogram."

Walking back to my cabin I realized I was already pregnant when we were in that road accident in Malaysia. Thankfully, I came out from that wreck without even a scratch. I was thrilled but also riddled with anxiety: "What if I have caused my baby to be deformed from the D&C?"

I immediately prayed and said, "Lord, I am so sorry. I didn't know I was already pregnant the very month I had another operation to find out why I wasn't getting pregnant."

It was one of those rare times that a scripture came straight to my mind, and I returned to these verses throughout my pregnancy. Philippians chapter 4, verses 6 and 7 say,

> Do not be anxious about anything, but in every situation, by prayer and petition, with thanksgiving, present your requests to God. And the peace of God, which transcends all understanding, will guard your hearts and your minds in Christ Jesus.

Once in Bangkok a few days later, I had the sonogram. The technician turned the screen around and showed me my tiny, tiny baby!

"You are not ten weeks pregnant; you are already thirteen weeks."

My spirits soared, "Oh my goodness, wow, thank you, Lord!"

Our baby was due March 26, 1988. Would you believe Roy and I had a conference to attend in Singapore on April 6, 1988? Our organization required us to be there, so I flew to Singapore six weeks before our baby was due.

I called the Singaporean gynecologist, the same doctor who had operated on me a month earlier, and told him the saga. He was taken aback, that was for sure. He admitted that he never ordered a blood test before he operated on me. He took full responsibility. I told him I was going to be in Singapore in March and asked him to deliver my baby. He said he would. No doctor is perfect, but he was a believer, and having a doctor who trusts in Jesus was enough for me.

For most of my pregnancy Roy and I were back in India. As I said, I flew to Singapore six weeks prior to my delivery date. An airline requirement is that no pregnant lady can fly after six weeks to her due date.

Once in Singapore I had the usual check-ups. All was well with my pregnancy up until our baby's expected due date. March 26th came and went. Not only did our baby not want to come out, the baby hadn't even dropped down in the engaged position. Dr. Chang, nonetheless, insisted my baby was ready to be born and called me in on March 31st to induce me. He put me on a drip to help my baby drop down and engage in the proper position.

After some time, since nothing was happening, the doctor said he was going to break my water. Wow, did that ever hurt. Now that the water was broken he expected my cervix to dilate. But he warned me that if it didn't, he would have to do a Caesarean and give me a general anesthetic.

"Oh, please don't give me a general anesthetic." I advocated for myself, "I've wanted a baby so much for so long and I want to be awake when my baby is born. Please give me an epidural." The epidural is an injection in the base of the spine to numb all feeling in that area of the body.

"Here in Singapore, women having a Caesarean always have a general," he countered.

I remained firm, "Well I'm not a Singaporean woman and I'm asking you to find someone who will give me an epidural. I want to be awake when my baby is born."

He left to look for a willing anesthetist. The first four he asked declined. The fifth, a female anesthetist, agreed to give me an epidural. Meanwhile, I was hooked up to a monitor listening to my baby's heartbeat. I was told that if it dropped below one hundred beats per minute, they would deliver my baby with an emergency Caesarean. Suddenly, the monitor showed the baby's heartbeat drop down to seventy beats per minute, and I was rushed into the delivery room for immediate surgery.

After I had a long needle inserted in the base of my spine, the epidural was done, and the doctor asked me if I was ready. An epidural requires a little time to take effect, and I could only say, "I will know that when the knife cuts my tummy."

"Can you feel this?" Dr. Chang asked.

"No, thankfully, I can't."

Within moments he had taken our baby girl out from within me.

"Is she alright?" was my first thought and question.

"She looks absolutely fine to me."

As soon as my little treasure was cleaned and wrapped up, a nurse put my baby in my arms. This was only for a few minutes, though, before she was taken away to be weighed and have the immediate baby checks. Soon I was back in my room, waiting for a nurse to wheel my baby beside me in a bassinette.

Oh, what happiness filled my heart to hold my little Lizzie! Words could not express my feelings of indescribable joy and thankfulness to God, my heavenly Father. I had no need to be anxious, as my beautiful little baby girl was resilient and survived all the obstacles that came her way. I loved breastfeeding her and having her nestle close to me.

It was during one of these moments that the thought came to me, "You will have another baby here in Singapore." Really, I didn't tell anyone. As Roy and I enjoyed those first few days, we just couldn't stop thanking God for giving us our precious little baby girl. I left the hospital on the sixth of April to go straight into a nice hotel where we attended a conference. Lizzie was perfectly happy sleeping peacefully in my arms.

30
A DELIGHTFUL SURPRISE

Three weeks later we were on a flight to Kathmandu. We wanted to be in India, but it was difficult to get a visa in the late eighties, so Roy attended a university in Kathmandu on a student visa to learn Sanskrit.

A few months later I said to Roy, "I think I am pregnant!" Sure enough, I was.

Immigration made a ruling that tourists could only stay in the country for six months of a year. Roy told me, "We can't go back to the States yet, so we will have to go back to Singapore and have this baby," and all I could do was smile.

Our son Paul was born on April 20th—his daddy's birthday—by Caesarean and by the same doctor who delivered Lizzie. It was a bit like having twins with two babies only one year and three weeks apart.

For the next eighteen years, until my children went off to college, I was in my element being a mother. Of course, even then I was still their mother, but they were young adults and somewhat independent of us. We raised our children in India. The four of us went back to the States for our children's college education in 2006.

While so much happened during those years, I have only one more incident I want to write about before drawing this testimony of God's goodness to a close.

Another Challenge

31
A BRAIN TUMOR

For four years we lived in California. While Paul was away at college and Lizzie was doing a study abroad semester in Delhi, Roy wanted to take me back to India in January of 2010 for a three-week visit.

Before leaving I decided to get new lenses in my glasses, since I thought my vision in my left eye was deteriorating. I told the optometrist I could see double out of my left eye. She told me to make an appointment to go see an ophthalmologist after I came back from India, which I did.

On March 20th when I went in for my appointment with the ophthalmologist, he took one look at my left eye and said it was protruding.

"Really, whatever do you suppose could be doing that?"

"A thyroid issue?" he suggested, knowing full well it was more likely to be a tumor.

"Please tell me the worst-case scenario," I probed.

He answered me directly with: "You could have a brain tumor and you need an MRI today."

An MRI did indeed reveal a tumor that had grown from the lining of my brain. The ophthalmologist arranged for me to see a brain surgeon. The brain surgeon showed Roy and me the MRI with a tumor sandwiched between my brain and left eye. The tumor was about to "hit" my optic nerve and make me blind in that eye.

I was told my tumor was a meningioma, which meant it was growing from the lining of my brain, and he was almost sure it was a benign tumor. He wanted to admit me to the hospital immediately and operate the next day.

He told us he would cut me from ear to ear and open my skull to get at the tumor and take out as much of it as possible.

"Can't we do this Monday? Do you know what weekend this is?" I asked.

"No, I don't know what weekend this is," the brain surgeon responded.

"It is Easter weekend and tomorrow is Good Friday," I told him.

While looking at Roy with some urgency, he replied, "It is entirely up to you."

Roy answered, "We will have Kelly admitted today and operate tomorrow."

The doctor gave us a paper with all the necessary blood tests to be done immediately and told us he would arrange for a bed for me in the hospital. That same evening, once I was hooked up with an intravenous, the surgeon came to see me and told me he needed me to have another MRI that night. I was surprised that I wasn't taken down to have that done until about 10:00 p.m.

While having the MRI, I started talking with Jesus. "Jesus, You know all about this tumor that has been growing for about twelve to fifteen years (so I was told by the doctor). All I can ask is that You will glorify Yourself in some way. I know You can dissolve or make this tumor go away. Wouldn't that surprise my doctor to see my MRI in the morning and see the tumor gone? Whatever You choose to do, I fully surrender myself again to You."

I came out of having the MRI at about 10:45 that night. No one was around, only the porter standing by a wheelchair ready to wheel me back to my room.

As I was about to sit in the chair, a man came walking towards me. When he came closer, I recognized that it was the brain surgeon who was to operate on me.

"Doctor, have you come to see me?"

"Yes, I have. Do you realize the severity of this operation?"

"Yes, I do."

"Do you know that you could have a stroke tomorrow while I operate?" he said.

"Yes, I guess I do, since I know two of my friends had strokes while they were having surgery."

"You could lose your eyesight," he continued. This was the first time I was taken aback.

"No, not my right eye; my right eye is my good eye."

"Yes, your right eye as well as your left eye."

Now I felt as though someone else was talking, even though the words were coming out of my mouth.

"In that case, doctor, you have come down to tell me at this late hour that I could die tomorrow."

He had no other word to tell me but "Yes."

I went on to say, "I highly esteem you for being a brain surgeon. I can hardly get my head around what you do; but I need to tell you that my life does not weigh in your balance. In fact, I would be a very foolish woman if I thought it.

"Whether I live or die tomorrow has already been decided by my Lord and Savior Jesus Christ. I have trusted in Him for the past thirty-eight years. Twenty-five of those years I have lived in India. Jesus was with me then and He is with me now."

I continued, "To be honest, I don't want to die. My children are not married yet and I would love to see them have children. But if that is not to be, then my Lord knows what is best for me. Whatever the outcome, I cannot lose."

He was looking at me intently as I went on. "If Jesus chooses to take me to my eternal home tomorrow, oh, what bliss that will be for me; if you are successful, then I may live another twenty years to testify of my Lord and Savior Jesus Christ."

After a short breath, I said, "And by now, my husband has emailed about three hundred friends and told them that I am having a six hour surgery tomorrow to take out as much of a meningioma brain tumor as possible; and I assure you, doctor, if they are praying for me, they will be praying for you."

And he said one word, "Really?"

"Yes, really and I want to thank you for coming to talk with me, but now it is late and I really want you to have a good night's sleep since I'm your first surgery tomorrow!"

The following morning the surgeon came to my bedside and said he could not operate because my blood was too thin, speaking in lay terms.

He wanted to know what medication I was taking. I told him none, only a laxative. It was the ginger in the laxative that caused my blood to be too thin to operate. He wrote me a prescription for steroids and seizure medicine and sent me home.

My operation was scheduled for a later date, by which time my blood would be thicker. For some reason, I asked Tina, who was on the neurologist's team, if I could talk to someone else and she suggested the tumor specialist who was going to assist the surgeon.

When we met, he told me that they would only be able to take out 10 percent of my tumor since my facial nerves and a major artery were running through the mass. This doctor suggested that while we were waiting for my blood to thicken, which could take up to four weeks or so, we should let the oncology and radiology department look at my MRIs and discuss with a brain surgeon if there could be an alternative treatment. All three decided that in my case my tumor could be shrunk with radiation.

My tumor was apparently very close to my optic nerve and they wanted to save the sight in my left eye. Yet that was not to be. While waiting for my radiation treatment to start, I lost sight in my left eye. I returned to the hospital immediately and had another MRI. The tumor specialist said there was nothing to worry about.

"Nothing to worry about," I thought, when I'd just gone blind in my left eye!

He continued to say that he would talk with the radiologist who was going to oversee my treatment to start radiation on me as soon as possible. I was to have thirty treatments of radiation. After thirteen days of treatment, light and very poor, blurred vision came back in my left eye.

To this day, more than eight years later, I do not see any better in my left eye; but I do see well with my right eye as long as I wear glasses. My tumor was supposed to shrink, but it never did. The radiation at least stopped the tumor from growing. Even though the plum-size tumor is still behind my left eye, I have never had a headache or any discomfort.

So, it was an excess of ginger in a laxative that saved me from having surgery. A couple of years ago, I was referred to a neurologist in India and while he was looking at my most recent MRI, which I have every year to make sure the tumor is not growing, he said, "I am so glad you did not have surgery on this tumor because you would not be in the good health that you are in now."

This comment made me think that the outcome, had I had surgery, would not have been pretty.

32
FINAL THOUGHTS

Before I return to Janini, the young girl I told you about at the beginning of my story, who had been so horribly abused and abandoned, I want to say in hindsight that being abandoned by Alan was the best thing that could have ever happened to me.

When he left me, I felt abandoned and alone. I had nowhere else to go but to God. God saw my heart, my hopeless state of mind, and how I felt altogether helpless and lost.

Let us revisit Janini. I said that if I had told you only her plight, there would have been little point in telling her story. As it happened, after she returned to Nepal, she was put in contact with a Nepali woman who loves Jesus and does what she can to take in and care for girls and young women who have been sold or kidnapped into prostitution.

That house mother of the girls is a dear friend of ours named Shanta who has given her life these past thirty years to care and see almost all of the one thousand girls come to know Jesus and have a relationship with Him. Each one of the girls has her own story; each one has survived her own nightmare. Shanta was there for them in the middle of the night when they woke up reliving the horror of what they survived. She knew she had nothing to offer them except the love of Jesus, which she gave through her own love and acceptance.

She provided a shoulder to cry on and a place to live and have their physical and spiritual needs met. In fact, the key to their healing was not about what she could offer them, but about what

Jesus Christ had already offered—that He had taken their pain and suffering upon the cross to become their Savior.

Sue, the founder of this home, is my friend who I met in Bombay and with whom I was on the same team during my second year in India. Sue was faithful to the call God put on her heart to build a home for abused girls who needed the love of Jesus Christ.

Shanta welcomed Janini into her home and heart when she was pregnant at fourteen years old. After all the pain and horror she had endured, Janini had a baby girl, Grace, who is now six years old.

It took a long time for Janini to recover. But with the love and support she found in the home, she surrendered her heart to Jesus. Now Janini knows she is a child of God. She knows she is valued and loved by her Savior and Lord, Jesus Christ, and has put her hope and trust in Him.

Dear reader, for those of us who have been abused sexually, physically, emotionally, mentally, we were the victims. Now we are survivors. The perpetrators, those who have wronged us, used us, and abused us, will be punished. Maybe you see them as free men or women today. Maybe they will not be brought to justice in this life, but there is One before whom they will have to stand—that One being Jesus Christ when the Day of Judgment comes. They will have to give an account before Him of what they have done in their life, including all the victims they abused or wronged in any way.

Consider allowing yourself to be set free now by the healing love and hope God offers us in His Son Jesus. Today, if you are safe from your abuser, if you have survived and overcome, do not let their chains of control extend into your life another day. Trust in God's justice and live free to become all God has made you to be.

I started my story when as a child I remembered asking myself, "What is the purpose and meaning of life?" Now, having lived sixty-seven years, I can honestly say that the purpose of life is to allow our Creator God to reside in our hearts, by His Holy Spirit, so that we might be led and guided by the only One who really knows how we can best live this life and honor Him. Once we are indwelt by God's Holy Spirit, we become free to allow God to live in and through us.

My dear friend, Jennifer, the daughter of Alan, with whom I was at school, emailed a few years ago and said, "You are not going to believe this. . ." (I thought, "Oh yes, I will!") ". . . but I too know Jesus Christ as my Savior and Lord."

I began to share Scripture with her, and she said, "Hey, slow down, you are ahead of me; you have had a relationship with Jesus for thirty-two years and I only for a few months."

Many people think that the Bible is an old, outdated book that has nothing to say to us today. In fact, the Bible has everything to say to us today. The Bible is about real people who lived real and messy lives. Everyone we read about in the Bible messed up in one way or another, all except One, Jesus Christ, who came to be the Savior of us all.

God is not going to intrude into your life, because He has given you free will. We all have to eat because God created us in such a way that food sustains us physically. He also created us with a spiritual need for Him so we would seek after Him and realize our very life relies on our being dependent on Him.

One of the most well-known verses in the Bible is John chapter 3 verse 16, "For God so loved the world that he gave his one and only Son, that whoever believes in him shall not perish but have eternal life."

God—the greatest giver

So loved—the greatest motive

The world—the greatest opportunity

That He gave His only Son—the greatest gift

That whosoever believes—the greatest invitation
Will not perish—the greatest freedom from destruction
But have eternal life—the greatest joy[1]

May I suggest that you get a Bible and start reading through the Gospel of John found in the New Testament. John was an apostle and a disciple of Jesus and spent three years with Him. In these twenty-one chapters, John tells us of Jesus and writes about Jesus' teaching and that Jesus is God in the flesh and that His ultimate reason for coming into the world was to be our Savior because we cannot save ourselves.

At the beginning of this book when I wrote about how I was searching for the meaning of life, I was also asking, "Won't someone love me for who I am, not for what they can get out of me?" I found that love in no other than Jesus Christ.

I will close now and allow the Holy Spirit to work in your hearts, because what I believed the Lord asked me to do in writing my story is finished, but His work is always ready to begin in your life. Once you get into reading the Word of God, the Bible, it teaches you about our Father God, His Son the Lord Jesus Christ, and His Holy Spirit, who is waiting to indwell you.

I am not talking religion—no, religion can amount to obeying rules. I am talking about having an exclusive relationship with God your Father, as well as your Friend, Savior, and Lord, Jesus Christ.

May God bless you, dear reader, as you seek to know your Lord and your God. I say farewell now with this Scripture found in Jeremiah chapter 29, verses 11–13:

---

1. Source unknown. This learning tool is commonly used and exists in various iterations.

'For I know the plans I have for you,' declares the
LORD, 'plans to prosper you and not to harm you,
plans to give you hope and a future. Then you will
call on me and come and pray to me, and I will
listen to you. You will seek me and find me when
you seek me with all your heart.'

Appendices

Appendix A
WHAT IS ABUSE?

Compiled by Hannah

You (or someone you love) may not realize you are a victim of abuse. Society tolerates the idea that abuse is limited to physical violence.

You may have had the thought: "He (or she) has never hit me, so while our relationship may not be perfect, I am not being abused." In fact, abuse covers a wide range of harmful dynamics.

Victims of abuse can be any age, gender, race, class, or religion, and abuse has many forms: *physical, emotional, verbal, sexual, financial, technological,* and *stalking.*

A common thread through each form of abuse is the dynamic of power and control. An abuser exerts power in order to control his or her victim. Abusers, however, can be charming and kind, especially at first. Abuse is not obvious, rather it can be subtle. This, plus many other factors, makes realizing you are a victim of abuse confusing; often the dynamics of an abusive relationship cloud a victim's thinking. Feelings of love can minimize the reality of a harmful relationship. Fear and shame, or even threats, keep victims silent. Isolation and lack of support can keep you from reaching out.

The following websites give detailed examples of what abuse is, who can be abused, and why it is very difficult for victims of abuse to get help. Their resources include insightful checklists, recommended booklists, and options to get support immediately. They offer free and confidential support, whether you need help to get safe or just speak with someone.

The resources here focus primarily on domestic or intimate partner abuse, which is abuse between two people who are supposed to be in a trusting, loving relationship. The dynamics may relate to but also differ from other types of abuse such as: child abuse, elder abuse, abuse of people with disabilities, or sexual assault.

No one deserves to be controlled by another person, or to live in fear and danger for their mind, body, emotions, finances, or loved ones. Abuse violates a person's identity at the deepest levels, whether it is violent in nature or otherwise insidious like verbal abuse (e.g. manipulation, put-downs, or threats).

You are not alone. A community exists and is ready to walk beside you toward safety, healing, and wholeness.

- **www.thehotline.org** The National Domestic Violence Hotline, known simply as *the Hotline*, has thorough resources for victims of abuse, as well as resources for people who work in the field.

- *The Hotline's* 24/7, free confidential support can be reached at 800-799-7233. They also have a live chat option so you can get support without saying a word.

- **www.loveisrespect.org** This site is designed for teens. In addition to addressing the main types of abuse, it gives ample attention to digital abuse and stalking. Love is Respect has a hotline for teens and a live chat option to use for immediate support, including talking about what a healthy relationship looks like: 866-331-9474.

- **https://www.rainn.org** RAINN (Rape, Abuse and Incest National Network), provides resources on sexual assault and abuse. This link **https://www.rainn.org/articles/adult-survivors-child-sexual-abuse** helps adult survivors process the long term impact of child sexual abuse. Their information provides healing guidance so one can process the past and face the future with hope. RAINN operates the *National Sexual Assault Hotline*, which is 24/7, free, and confidential: 800-656-HOPE.

Appendix B
WHAT DOES THE BIBLE SAY ABOUT ABUSE AND ABUSERS?

Below are some Bible verses with special relevance to us as victims. Some verses regard how God views perpetrators and what awaits them. Others offer us hope as we move from being victims to survivors living with hope and purpose.

> For we must all appear before the judgment seat of Christ, so that each of us may receive what is due us for the things done while in the body, whether good or bad. (2 Corinthians 5:10)

> God "will repay each person according to what they have done." To those who by persistence in doing good seek glory, honor and immortality, he will give eternal life. But for those who are self-seeking and who reject the truth and follow evil, there will be wrath and anger. (Romans 2:6–8)

> The LORD is in his holy temple; the LORD is on his heavenly throne. He observes everyone on earth; his eyes examine them. The LORD examines the righteous, but the wicked, those who love violence, he hates with a passion. On the wicked he will rain fiery coals and burning sulfur; a scorching wind will be their lot. For the LORD is

righteous, he loves justice; the upright will see his face. (Psalm 11:4–7)

Do not take revenge, my dear friends, but leave room for God's wrath, for it is written: "It is mine to avenge; I will repay," says the Lord. (Romans 12:19)

The LORD is a refuge for the oppressed, a stronghold in times of trouble. Those who know your name will trust in you, for you, LORD, have never forsaken those who seek you . . . For he who avenges blood remembers; he does not ignore the cry of the afflicted. (Psalm 9:9–11)

Therefore, if anyone is in Christ, the new creation has come: The old has gone, the new is here! (2 Corinthians 5:17)

Appendix C
CHRISTIAN RESOURCES
ON HEALING FROM ABUSE

Compiled by Hannah

The story you have just read is one example of a woman's journey from desolation to wholeness. Kelly found value, freedom, purpose, and love in her Savior and Friend, Jesus. Survivors' paths take a variety of routes, with the role of faith and God being different for each one.

It is possible that religion has been a source of control and shaming in your abusive relationship. Perhaps at one time you, or your loved one, reached out to a trusted leader, such as a pastor or priest, and were told to stay or pray your way through your situation. Often society, including faith communities, have sided with or turned a blind eye to abusers. Scriptures have been used historically to justify rather than correct oppressors' actions. That may be part of your experience.

As more and more survivors break their silence, however, faith communities are becoming informed and are learning how to stand up for justice by standing with survivors of abuse.

Kelly's story gives witness to the reality that a personal faith in Jesus is a powerful yet gentle source of healing. We know Jesus as not only Savior and Friend, but also as Defender, Advocate, Healer, and Hope.

As you explore the resources in Appendix A and gain strength as a survivor of abuse, use the following resources from Christian sources on healing from abuse. May you find empowerment for your journey of healing to become all that you are meant to be.

- **https://www.focusonthefamily.com/
  lifechallenges/abuse-and-addiction/
  understanding-emotional-abuse/under-
  standing-emotional-abuse** Focus on the
  Family has a six part series of short articles
  dealing with abuse, healing and faith. You can
  hear broadcasts or read the transcripts of shows
  covering a helpful range from domestic violence
  in Christian homes and the church to surviving
  child sexual abuse, including how to support a
  spouse who is a survivor.

- **https://godswordtowomen.org/healing_
  Boone.htm** This survivor and pastor in North
  Carolina shares her story of childhood suffering
  that culminated in greater pain and destruction
  but that ultimately led her to her Jesus encounter. She recognizes that coming to faith in Christ
  is only one step in the healing journey and that
  ongoing work is needed. She also addresses the
  fact that so many people sitting in the church
  pews, suffer in silence—statistically as many as
  one in four.

- **https://www.leslievernick.com/how-do-
  i-heal-from-emotional-abuse** Leslie Vernick's
  website is dedicated to issues of healing from
  abuse, addiction, and destructive relationships.
  She is a Christian counselor and survivor.

- **https://www.reviveourhearts.com/radio/
  revive-our-hearts/healing-years-abuse** Listen
  to or read the transcript of Josh McDowell's
  testimony of surviving sexual abuse and his

childhood in an alcoholic home. He considers how, many years later, as an adult, Jesus' love saved him from hating his absent alcoholic father and the trusted worker on his family's farm who sexually abused him for seven years. This is part of a bigger series on abuse.

- **https://www.todayschristianwoman.com/ articles/2008/september/opening-door- to-healing.html** This article examines how childhood sexual abuse later affects marital intimacy, through the author's story and research. Her husband writes a short piece at the end discussing their trials and triumphs from his point of view.

- **http://www.hiddenhurt.co.uk/religion_ and_domestic_violence.html** This speaks directly to victims of domestic abuse within the Christian church. It explains the biblical view of abuse and provides detailed support and resources on abuse in general for survivors and people who support them.